Advancing Maths for AQA
STATISTICS 5

Roger Williamson, Gill Buqué, Jim Miller and Chris Worth

Series editors
Roger Williamson   Sam Boardman
Ted Graham   Keith Parramore

Heinemann Educational Publishers
a division of Heinemann Publishers (Oxford) Ltd,
Halley Court, Jordan Hill, Oxford OX2 8EJ

OXFORD   MELBOURNE   AUCKLAND   JOHANNESBURG   IBADAN
BLANTYRE   GABORONE   PORTSMOUTH NH (USA)   CHICAGO

First published in 2002

04 03 02
10 9 8 7 6 5 4 3 2 1

ISBN 0 435 513 168

Cover design by Miller, Craig and Cocking

Typeset and illustrated by Tech-Set Limited, Gateshead, Tyne & Wear

Printed and bound by Scotprint in the UK

Acknowledgements
The publishers and authors acknowledge the work of the writers, David Cassell,
Ian Hardwick, Mary Rouncefield, David Burghes, Ann Ault and Nigel Price of
the *AEB Mathematics for AS* and *A-Level series*, from which some exercises and
examples have been taken.

The authors and publishers would like to thank Elsevier Science for permission
to use the data in Q7 p. 141, which is taken from *The Lancet* Vol 348, No 9035,
1996.

The publishers' and authors' thanks are due to the AQA for permission to
reproduce questions from past examination papers.

The answers have been provided by the authors and are not the responsibility
of the examining board.

About this book

This book is one in a series of textbooks designed to provide you with exceptional preparation for AQA's new Advanced GCE Specification B. The series authors are all senior members of the examining team and have prepared the textbooks specifically to support you in studying this course.

S5 is an A2 unit in statistics without a prerequisite AS unit. It is designed for candidates who wish to study A level mathematics with two applications. Thus four pure mathematics units can be combined with an AS unit in discrete mathematics or mechanics and an A2 unit in statistics to make up A level mathematics. In order to produce a viable A2 unit without prerequisite it has been necessary to assume that candidates will be familiar from their GCSE studies with numerical measures – most importantly mean and standard deviation – and with diagrammatic representation of data. This book consists of the material from the books covering units S1 and S4 which is relevant to the S5 specification. There is one chapter for each section of the specification together with a brief introductory chapter. The first chapter deals with some ideas which are fundamental to understanding statistics but which will not be examined directly in the examination.

Finding your way around

The following are there to help you find your way around when you are studying and revising:

- **edge marks** (shown on the front page) – these help you to get to the right chapter quickly;

- **contents list** – this identifies the individual sections dealing with key syllabus concepts so that you can go straight to the areas that you are looking for;

- **index** – a number in bold type indicates where to find the main entry for that topic.

Key points

Key points are not only summarised at the end of each chapter but are also boxed and highlighted within the text like this:

A **parameter** is a numerical property of a **population** and a **statistic** is a numerical property of a **sample**.

Exercises and exam questions

Worked examples and carefully graded questions familiarise you with the specification and bring you up to exam standard. Each book contains:

- Worked examples and Worked exam questions to show you how to tackle typical questions; Examiner's tips will also provide guidance;

- Graded exercises, gradually increasing in difficulty up to exam-level questions, which are marked by an [A];

- Test-yourself sections for each chapter so that you can check your understanding of the key aspects of that chapter and identify any sections that you should review;

- Answers to the questions are included at the end of the book.

7 Hypothesis testing

Exam style practice paper

Appendix

Answers

Index

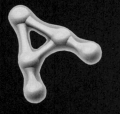

CHAPTER I

Collection of data

Learning objectives

After studying this chapter, you should be able to:
- identify different types of variable and to distinguish between primary and secondary data
- understand the terms population, sample, parameter, statistic
- use random digits to select a random sample.

1.1 Introduction

This chapter deals with some basic statistical ideas which are not explicitly in the specification but which are fundamental to the understanding of statistics.

1.2 What is statistics?

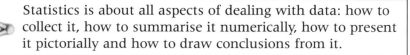

> Statistics is about all aspects of dealing with data: how to collect it, how to summarise it numerically, how to present it pictorially and how to draw conclusions from it.

Statistics deals with events which have more than one possible outcome. If you buy a sandwich, in a canteen, priced at £1.20 and offer the cashier a £5 note you should receive £3.80 in change. This is not statistics as there is (or should be) only one amount of change possible.

If the canteen manager wishes to know how much customers spend when visiting the canteen, this is statistics because different customers spend different amounts.

The quantity which varies – in this case the amount of money – is called a **variable**.

Who uses statistics?

- Car manufacturers: to ensure components meet specification.
- Doctors: to compare the results of different treatments for the same condition.
- Government: to plan provision of schools and health services.
- Scientists: to test their theories.
- Opinion pollsters: to find the public's opinion on local or national issues.

Types of variables

Qualitative variables

There are a number of different types of variables.

> **Qualitative variables** do not have a numerical value. Place of birth, sex of a baby and colour of car are all qualitative variables.

Quantitative variables

> **Quantitative variables** do have a numerical value. They can be **discrete** or **continuous**.

- **Discrete variables** take values which change in steps:

The number of eggs a hen lays in a week can only take whole number values. **Discrete** means separate – there are no possible values in between.

Variables which are counted, such as the number of cars crossing a bridge in a minute, are discrete, but discrete variables are not limited to whole number values. For example, if a sample of five components are examined, the proportion which fail to meet the specifications is a discrete variable which can take the values 0, 0.2, 0.4, 0.6, 0.8 and 1.

- **Continuous variables** can take any value in an interval. For example, height of a child, length of a component or weight of an apple. Such variables are measured, not counted.

A lizard could be 12 cm long, or 12.5 cm, or any length in between. In practice length will be measured to a given accuracy, say the nearest millimetre. Only certain values will be possible, but in theory there is no limit to the number of different possible lengths.

Sometimes variables which are strictly discrete may be treated as continuous. Money changes in steps of 1p and so is a discrete variable. However, if you are dealing with hundreds of pounds the steps are so small that it may be treated as a continuous variable.

Primary and secondary data

A vast amount of data on a wide variety of topics is published by the Government and other organisations. Much of it appears in publications such as *Monthly Digest of Statistics, Social Trends* and *Annual Abstract of Statistics*. These will provide useful data for many investigations. These data are known as **secondary** data as they were not collected specifically for the investigation. Data which are collected for a specific investigation are known as **primary** data.

> There are questions on secondary data in module S2. For this module all you need to know is the difference between primary and secondary data.

EXERCISE 1A

1 Classify each of the following variables as either qualitative, discrete quantitative or continuous quantitative.

   (a) Colours of roses.

   (b) Numbers of bicycles owned by families in Stockport.

   (c) Ages of students at a college.

   (d) Volumes of contents of vinegar bottles.

   (e) Countries of birth of British citizens.

   (f) Numbers of strokes to complete a round of golf.

   (g) Proportions of faulty valves in samples of size ten.

   (h) Diameters of cricket balls.

   (i) Prices, in £, of chocolate bars.

   (j) Makes of car in a car park.

1.3 Populations and samples

What is the average height of women in the UK? To find out you could, in theory, measure them all. In practice this would be impossible. Fortunately you don't need to. Instead you can measure the heights of a sample. Provided the sample is carefully chosen you can obtain almost as much information from the sample as from measuring the height of every woman in the UK.

In statistics we distinguish between a **population** and a **sample**.

> A **population** is all the possible data and a **sample** is part of the data.

The **population** is all the possible data

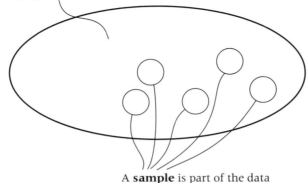

A **sample** is part of the data

The difference between a population and a sample is of great importance in later statistics modules.

Sampling is useful because it reduces the amount of data you need to collect and process. It also allows you to carry out a test without affecting all the population. For example the contents of a sample of tubs of margarine, from a large batch, might be weighed to ensure that the actual contents matched that claimed on the label. Emptying the tubs to weigh the margarine makes them unsaleable, so it would be ridiculous to weigh the contents of the whole population of tubs.

A numerical property of a population is called a **parameter**. A numerical property of a sample is called a **statistic**. For example, the proportion of tubs in the consignment containing more than 450 g of margarine is a parameter, while the proportion in the sample is a statistic. Similarly, the mean height of all adult females in the UK is a parameter, while the mean height of the adult females in the sample is a statistic.

> A **parameter** is a numerical property of a **population** and a **statistic** is a numerical property of a **sample**.

EXERCISE 1B

1 Read the following passage and identify an example of:
  (a) a population,
  (b) a sample,
  (c) a parameter,
  (d) a statistic,
  (e) a qualitative variable,
  (f) a discrete variable,
  (g) a continuous variable,
  (h) primary data,
  (i) secondary data.

A South American sports journalist intends to write a book about football in his home country. He will analyse all first division matches in the season. He records for each match whether it is a home win, an away win or a draw. He also records for each match the total number of goals scored and the amount of time played before a goal is scored. Reference books showed that in the previous season the mean number of goals per game was 2.317. On the first Saturday of the season he recorded the number of goals scored in each match and calculated the mean number of goals per match as 2.412. For the whole season the mean number of goals per match was 2.219.

2 Read the following paragraph:

'All pupils at Gortincham High School undergo a medical examination during their first year at the school. The data recorded for each pupil include place of birth, sex, age (in years and months), height and weight. A summary of the data collected is available on request. A class of statistics students decides to collect data on the weight of second year pupils and compare them with the data on first year pupils. It is agreed that the data will be collected one lunchtime. Each member of the class will be provided with a set of bathroom scales and will weigh as many second year pupils as possible. At the end of the lunchtime they will each report the number of pupils weighed and the mean of the weights recorded.'

In the paragraph you have just read identify:
  (a) **two** qualitative variables,
  (b) **two** continuous variables,
  (c) **one** discrete quantitative variable,
  (d) secondary data,
  (e) primary data,
  (f) a population,
  (g) a sample,
  (h) a statistic.

1.4 Sampling without bias

When you are selecting a sample you need to avoid **bias** – anything which makes the sample unrepresentative. For example, if you want to estimate how often residents of Manchester visit the cinema in a year it would be foolish to stand outside a cinema as the audience is coming out and ask people as they pass. This would give a biased sample as all the people you ask would have been to the cinema at least once that year. You can avoid bias by taking a random sample.

Sampling is a major topic in module S2. In this module you only need to know about random sampling.

Random sampling

For a sample to be random every member of the population must have an equal chance of being selected. However, this alone is not sufficient. If the population consists of 10 000 heights and a random sample of size 20 is required then every possible set of 20 heights must have an equal chance of being chosen.

For example, suppose the population consists of the heights of 100 students in a college and you wish to take a sample of size 5. The students' names are arranged in alphabetical order and numbered 00 to 99. A number between 00 and 19 is selected by lottery methods. For example, place 20 equally sized balls numbered 00 to 19 in a bag and ask a blindfolded assistant to pick one out. This student and every 20th one thereafter are chosen and their heights measured. That is, if the number 13 is selected then the students numbered 13, 33, 53, 73 and 93 are chosen. Every student would have an equal chance of being chosen. However, a sister and brother who were next to each other in the alphabetical list could never both be included in the same sample, so this is **not** a random sample.

> Not every set of five students could be chosen.

Usually, if you decide to choose five students at random you intend to choose five different students and would not consider choosing the same student twice. This is known as sampling without replacement.

A random sample chosen without replacement is called a **simple random sample**. If you did allow the possibility of a member of the population being chosen more than once this would be sampling with replacement. A random sample chosen with replacement is called an **unrestricted random sample**.

Random numbers

The previous section referred to numbers being selected by lottery methods. In practice it is much more convenient to use random numbers. These are numbers which have been generated so that each digit from 0 to 9 has an equal chance of appearing in each position. They may be obtained from your calculator or from tables. An extract from random number tables is shown on page 7.

> Your calculator may generate random numbers between 0 and 1, say 0.206. To turn these into random digits ignore 0. and use 206.

Worked example 1.1

Describe how random numbers could be used to select a simple random sample of size 7 from the 63 residents of Mandela Close who are on the electoral register.

Solution

First number the residents. This is easy as a list of names is already available in the electoral register.

00	Chuzzlewit, M
01	Ngo, S
02	Sodiwala, V
03	Shah, D
04	O'Shea, M

You could place a number by each name, or simply decide that the top name will be 00, the next 01 and so on.

Next choose any starting point in the random number tables.

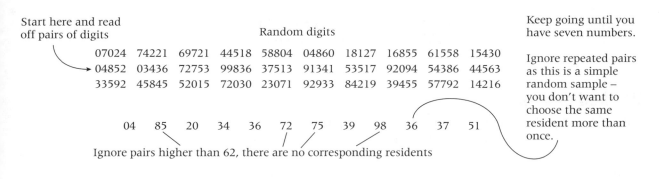

Start here and read off pairs of digits — Random digits — Keep going until you have seven numbers.

```
07024  74221  69721  44518  58804  04860  18127  16855  61558  15430
04852  03436  72753  99836  37513  91341  53517  92094  54386  44563
33592  45845  52015  72030  23071  92933  84219  39455  57792  14216
```

Ignore repeated pairs as this is a simple random sample – you don't want to choose the same resident more than once.

```
04   85   20   34   36   72   75   39   98   36   37   51
```

Ignore pairs higher than 62, there are no corresponding residents

When you have seven different numbers in the range 00 to 62, use them to choose the corresponding residents.

> You could have numbered from 01 to 63. In this case you would have to ignore 00 and numbers greater than 63.

```
04   20   34   36   39   37   51
```

O'Shea

Worked example 1.2 _____

A trade union wished to ask a sample of 100 members to answer a questionnaire about the services it provides. A list of all the 98 650 members of the union is obtained and numbered from 00 000 to 98 649.

Five digit random numbers are read from a table and any numbers over 98 649 are ignored. This continues until 100 five digit numbers have been obtained. The corresponding union members are contacted with a request to complete the questionnaire.

(a) What is the name given to this method of sampling?

(b) How would this method of sampling be modified if a simple random sample was required?

(c) Which of these two methods of sampling would you recommend?

Solution

(a) This is an **unrestricted random sample**.

(b) The method would be the same except that any repeated random numbers would be ignored. This would prevent the same union member being selected twice.

(c) There is no purpose in asking the same union member to fill in a questionnaire twice and so a simple random sample would be preferred. (However, as the sample is small compared to the population it is, in this case, very unlikely that the same member would have been selected more than once.)

Worked example 1.3

Following a spell of particularly bad weather, an insurance company received 42 claims for storm damage on the same day. Sufficient staff were available to investigate only six of these claims. The others would be paid in full without investigation. The claims were numbered 00 to 41 and the following suggestions were made as to the method used to select the six. In each case six different claims are required, so any repeats would be ignored.

Method 1 Choose the six largest claims.

Method 2 Select two digit random numbers, ignoring any greater than 41. When six have been obtained, choose the corresponding claims.

Method 3 Select two digit random numbers. Divide each one by 42, take the remainder and choose the corresponding claims (e.g. if 44 is selected, claim number 02 would be chosen).

Method 4 As 3, but when selecting the random numbers ignore 84 and over.

Method 5 Select a single digit at random, ignoring 7 and over. Choose this and every seventh claim thereafter (e.g. if 3 is selected, choose claims numbered 03, 10, 17, 24, 31 and 38).

Comment on each of the methods including an explanation of whether it would yield a random sample or not.

Solution

Method 1. This would be a sensible policy for the insurance company to adopt but it would not be a random sample. The smaller claims have no chance of being chosen.

Method 2. This is exactly the method we have used in Worked example 1.1 and would yield a random sample.

Method 3. This would not give all claims an equal chance of being chosen. For example, the claim numbered 01 would be included in the sample if 01, 43 or 85 were selected. However, the claim numbered 30 would only be included if 30 or 72 were selected.

> Some claims would have two chances of being included, others would have three chances.

Method 4. This would yield a random sample. All claims would have two numbers associated with them and so have an equal chance of being chosen. In the example in method 3 the claim numbered 01 is now only chosen if 01 or 43 were selected.

Method 5. Each claim would have an equal chance of being selected but this would not be a random sample as not all combinations of six claims could be chosen.

> This is an unnecessarily complicated method but has the advantage that less two digit random numbers are rejected as too high than in method 2. It might be useful if there were, say, 1050 items in the population numbered 0000 to 1049. Four digit random numbers would be needed but the great majority would be out of the required range.

EXERCISE 1C

1 On a particular day there are 2125 books on the shelves in the fiction section of a library. Describe how random numbers could be used to select a random sample of size 20 (without replacement) from the 2125 books. [A]

2 Describe how random numbers could be used to select a simple random sample of size 6 from the 712 employees of a large city centre store. [A]

3 A gardener grew 28 tomato plants. Describe how you would use random numbers to take a simple random sample of size 8 from the population. [A]

4 The ages, in years, of the students in a statistics class are given below.

19 20 23 21 21 20 20 19 19 20 19 24
20 19 20 22 21 25 20 33 19 19 19 20
49 24 36 27 33 26 38 43 24 41 30 27

Explaining fully the procedure you use, take:
   (a) an unrestricted random sample (i.e. allow the same student to be chosen more than once) of size 6 from the population,
   (b) a simple random sample (i.e. do not allow the same student to be chosen more than once) of size 6 from the population. [A]

5 Describe how a simple random sample of 20 rods could be taken from a population of 500 rods. [A]

6 In order to estimate the mean number of books borrowed by members of a public library, the librarian decides to record the number of books borrowed by a sample of 40 members. She chooses the first member of the sample by selecting a random integer, r, between 1 and 5 inclusive. She then includes in her sample the rth member to leave the library one morning and every 5th member to leave after that until her sample of 40 is complete. Thus, if $r = 3$ she chooses the 3rd, 8th, 13th, ..., 198th members leaving the library as her sample.

(a) Does the sample constitute a random sample of the first 200 people leaving the library? Give a reason.

(b) A list of the names of the 8950 members of the library is available. Describe how random sampling numbers could be used to select a random sample (without replacement) of 40 of these names. [A]

7 In a particular parliamentary constituency there are 64 000 names on the electoral register. Of the electors, 32 000 live in property rented from the local authority, 21 000 live in owner-occupied property and 11 000 live in other types of property.

A total of 64 electors are selected at random from those living in property rented from the local authority, 42 electors are selected at random from those living in owner-occupied property and 22 electors are selected at random from those living in the other types of property. State, giving a reason, whether a random sample of electors has been selected.

Key point summary

1 **Statistics** is about all aspects of dealing with data. *p1*

2 **Qualitative variables** do not have a numerical value. *p2*

3 **Discrete quantitative variables** take values which change in steps. *p2*

4 **Continuous quantitative variables** can take any value in an interval. *p2*

5 A **population** is all the data. *p3*

6 A **sample** is part of the data. *p3*

7 A **parameter** is a numerical property of a population. *p4*

8 A **statistic** is a numerical property of a sample. *p4*

9 A **random sample** of size n is a sample selected so that all possible samples of size n have an equal chance of being selected. *p6*

10 **Simple** random samples are selected without replacement, **unrestricted** random samples are selected with replacement. *p6*

Test yourself	What to review
1 Explain the difference between a population and a sample.	*Section 1.1*
2 State the type of each of the following variables:	*Section 1.1*
(a) time you have to wait to see a doctor in a casualty department,	
(b) colour of eyes,	
(c) proportion of rainy days in a given week.	
3 Explain the difference between a statistic and a parameter.	*Section 1.2*
4 An inspector tests every 100th assembly coming off a production line. Explain why this is not a random sample of the assemblies.	*Section 1.3*
5 Explain the difference between primary and secondary data.	*Section 1.1*

Test yourself ANSWERS

1 A population is all the data, a sample is part of the data.

2 (a) Continuous quantitative;

   (b) Qualitative;

   (c) Discrete quantitative.

3 A statistic is a numerical property of a sample, a parameter is a numerical property of a population.

4 Not all combinations of assemblies could be included in the sample. For example two adjacent assemblies could not both be sampled.

5 Primary data are data collected specifically for a particular investigation, secondary data may be used in the investigation but were not collected specifically for this purpose.

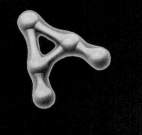

CHAPTER 2
Probability

Learning objectives

After studying this chapter you should be able to:
- understand the concept of probability and be able to allocate probabilities using equally likely outcomes
- identify mutually exclusive events and independent events
- apply the law $P(A \text{ or } B) = P(A) + P(B)$ to mutually exclusive events
- apply the law $P(A \text{ and } B) = P(A)P(B)$ to independent events or the law $P(A \text{ and } B) = P(A)P(B|A)$ to events which are not independent
- solve simple probability problems using tree diagrams or the laws of probability.

2.1 Probability

The concept of probability is widely understood. For example, Courtney might say that the probability of having to wait more than 5 minutes for a bus on a weekday morning is 0.4. He means that if he carries out a large number of **trials** (that is, he waits for a bus on a large number of weekday mornings) he expects to have to wait more than 5 minutes in about 0.4 or 40% of these **trials**.

Probability is measured on a scale from 0 to 1. Zero represents impossibility and 1 represents certainty.

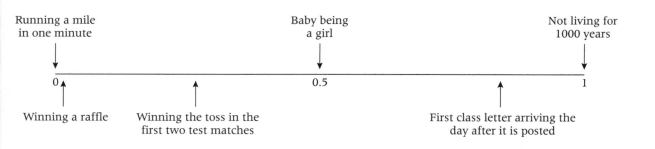

2.2 Equally likely outcomes

Often trials can result in a number of equally likely outcomes. For example, if there are 25 people in a room and a trial consists of choosing one at random there are 25 equally likely outcomes.

An **event** consists of one or more of the outcomes. Choosing a particular person, choosing someone wearing glasses or choosing a male would all be examples of events.

If Janice is one of the people in the room then the probability of the event 'choosing Janice' occurring as a result of the trial is $\frac{1}{25}$.

If there are six people wearing glasses in the room the probability of the event 'choosing someone wearing glasses' occurring as a result of the trial is $\frac{6}{25}$.

> You will understand what is meant by 'equally likely'. Don't try to give it a precise definition – it can't be done.

If a trial can result in one of n equally likely outcomes and an event consists of r of these outcomes, then the probability of the event happening as a result of the trial is $\frac{r}{n}$.

> It must be impossible for more than one of the outcomes to occur as a result of the same trial.

Worked example 2.1

If a fair die is thrown, what is the probability that it lands showing: **(a)** 2, **(b)** an even number, **(c)** more than 4?

Solution

There are six equally likely outcomes. The probability of any one of them occurring is therefore $\frac{1}{6}$.

(a) $P(2) = \frac{1}{6}$;

(b) $P(\text{even number}) = P(2, 4 \text{ or } 6) = \frac{3}{6} = \frac{1}{2}$;

(c) $P(\text{more than } 4) = P(5 \text{ or } 6) = \frac{1}{3}$.

EXERCISE 2A

1 A box contains 20 counters, numbered 1, 2, 3, …, 20. A counter is taken out of the box. What is the probability that it: **(a)** is the number 7, **(b)** is a multiple of 4, **(c)** is greater than 14, **(d)** has a 3 on it?

2 The days of the week are written on seven separate cards. One card is chosen. What is the probability that it is: **(a)** Thursday, **(b)** either Monday or Tuesday, **(c)** not Friday, Saturday or Sunday?

3 In a word game, Charlie has the letters B, E, E, H, Q, S, and T. One letter accidentally falls on to the floor. What is the probability that it is:

(a) Q, (b) B, E or S, (c) not an E?

4 In a box there are 15 beads. Seven are white, three are yellow, three are blue and two are green. If one bead is selected at random, what is the probability that it is: (a) white, (b) yellow or green, (c) not blue, (d) brown, (e) neither white nor yellow?

5 A cricket team has five batters, a wicketkeeper, three bowlers and two all-rounders. One player is selected at random to pack the cricket bag. What is the probability that the selected player is: (a) the wicketkeeper, (b) a bowler, (c) not an all-rounder, (d) neither a batter nor a bowler?

2.3 Relative frequency

It is not always possible to assign a probability using equally likely outcomes. For example, when Courtney waits for a bus he either has to wait for less than 5 minutes or for 5 or more minutes. However, there is no reason to think that these two outcomes are equally likely. In this case the only way to assign a probability is to carry out the trial a large number of times and to see how often a particular outcome occurs. If Courtney went for a bus on 40 weekday mornings and on 16 of these he had to wait more than 5 minutes he could assign the probability 16/40 = 0.4 to the event of having to wait more than 5 minutes.

The **relative frequency** of an event is the proportion of times it has been observed to happen.

The **relative frequency** method of assigning probabilities suffers from the problem that if Courtney carried out a large number of further trials it is not possible to prove that the relative frequency would not change completely. However, when this method has been used in practice it has always happened that although the relative frequency may fluctuate over the first few trials, these fluctuations become small after a large number of trials.

> In examination questions you will either be given the probability of an event or be required to find it using equally likely outcomes.

In all cases where equally likely outcomes can be used it is also possible to use the relative frequency method. When this has been done it has always been observed that provided a large number of trials are carried out the two methods give very similar although not quite identical results. For example, when a die has been thrown a large number of times the proportion of 1s observed is very close to $\frac{1}{6}$.

2.4 Mutually exclusive events

> When you pick a card from a pack, it must be a club, diamond, heart or a spade. The card cannot be, say, both a club and a heart. The events 'picking a club', 'picking a diamond', 'picking a heart' and 'picking a spade' are said to be **mutually exclusive**. The occurrence of one event **excludes** the possibility that any of the other events could occur.

Worked example 2.2

One card is selected from a pack. Which of these pairs of events are mutually exclusive?

(a) 'The card is a heart' and 'the card is a spade'.

(b) 'The card is a club' and 'the card is a Queen'.

(c) 'The card is black' and 'the card is a diamond'.

(d) 'The card is a King' and 'the card is an Ace'.

(e) 'The card is red' and 'the card is a heart'.

Solution

(a), **(c)** and **(d)**.

In **(b)** it is possible to have a card which is **both** a club **and** a Queen (the Queen of Clubs), and in **(e)** a red card could be a heart.

In **(a)**, **(c)** and **(d)** the two events cannot occur simultaneously, hence they are mutually exclusive.

The pack of 52 cards contains 13 clubs, 13 diamonds, 13 hearts and 13 spades. The probability of picking a club is $\frac{13}{52} = 0.25$. The probability of picking a diamond is $\frac{13}{52} = 0.25$. The probability of picking a club or a diamond is $\frac{26}{52} = 0.5$. This is equal to the probability of picking a club plus the probability of picking a diamond. This is an example of the addition law of probability **as it applies to mutually exclusive events**.

> If A and B are mutually exclusive events then the probability of A or B occurring as a result of a trial is the sum of the separate probabilities of A and B occurring as a result of the trial.
>
> $$\mathbf{P}(A \text{ or } B) = \mathbf{P}(A) + \mathbf{P}(B)$$

This law can be extended to more than two mutually exclusive events. For example the probability of picking a club, a diamond or a heart is $0.25 + 0.25 + 0.25 = 0.75$.

P(A or B) denotes the probability of A or B or both occurring. However, here we are dealing with mutually exclusive events so A and B cannot both occur.

If A and B are not mutually exclusive the law is more complicated. You will not need the more complicated form in this module and rarely need it in other modules.

P(A or B or C)
= P(A) + P(B) + P(C)

A person, selected at random from 25 people in a room, must either be wearing glasses or not wearing glasses. These two events are mutually exclusive, but one of them must happen. One of these events is called the **complement** of the other. The complement of event A is usually denoted A'.

Another way of saying that one of the events must happen is to say the events are **exhaustive**.

2

As one of the events must happen $P(A \text{ or } A') = 1$.

As the events are mutually exclusive
$P(A) + P(A') = P(A \text{ or } A') = 1$
or $P(A') = 1 - P(A)$

Sometimes it is much easier to work out P(A) than P(A′) or vice versa. You can find whichever is easier and, if necessary, use this rule to find the other.

EXERCISE 2B

1 The probability of Brian passing a driving test is 0.6. Write down the probability of him not passing the test.

2 The probability of a TV set requiring repair within 1 year is 0.22. Write down the probability of a TV set not requiring repair within 1 year.

3 When Devona rings her mother the probability that the phone is engaged is 0.1, the probability that the phone is not engaged but no one answers is 0.5 and the probability that the phone is answered is 0.4.

Find the probability that:

(a) the phone is engaged or no one answers, **(b)** the phone is engaged or it is answered, **(c)** the phone is not engaged.

4 Kofi shops exactly once a week. In a particular week the probability that he shops on a Monday is 0.3, on a Tuesday is 0.4 and on a Wednesday is 0.1.

Find the probability that he goes shopping on:

(a) Monday or Tuesday, **(b)** Monday or Wednesday,
(c) Monday or Tuesday or Wednesday, **(d)** not on Monday,
(e) Thursday or Friday or Saturday or Sunday.

5 There are 35 customers in a canteen, 12 are aged over 50, 15 are aged between 30 and 50 and five are aged between 25 and 29.

Find the probability that the next customer to be served is aged:

(a) 30 or over, **(b)** 25 or over, **(c)** under 25, **(d)** 50 or under.

6 Charlotte is expecting a baby:

A is the event that the baby will have blue eyes;

B is the event that the baby will have green eyes;

C is the event that the baby will have brown hair.

(a) Write down two of these events which are:

(i) mutually exclusive, **(ii)** not mutually exclusive.

(b) Define the complement of event *A*.

7 A firm employs 20 bricklayers. The Inland Revenue selects one for investigation:

A is the event that the bricklayer selected earned less than £20 000 last year;

B is the event that the bricklayer selected earned more than £20 000 last year;

C is the event that the bricklayer selected earned £20 000 or more last year.

(a) Which event is the complement of *C*?

(b) Are the events *A* and *B* mutually exclusive?

(c) Write down two of the events which are not mutually exclusive.

2.5 Independent events

When the probability of event *A* occurring is unaffected by whether or not event *B* occurs the two events are said to be **independent**.

For example, if event *A* is throwing an even number with a blue die and event *B* is throwing an odd number with a red die, then the probability of event *A* is $\frac{3}{6} = 0.5$ regardless of whether or not event *B* occurs. Events *A* and *B* are independent.

If two dice are thrown there are 36 equally likely possible outcomes:

1,1	1,2	1,3	1,4	1,5	1,6
2,1	2,2	2,3	2,4	2,5	2,6
3,1	3,2	3,3	3,4	3,5	3,6
4,1	4,2	4,3	4,4	4,5	4,6
5,1	5,2	5,3	5,4	5,5	5,6
6,1	6,2	6,3	6,4	6,5	6,6

If you wish to find the probability of the total score being 12 you can observe that only one of the outcomes (6,6) gives a total score of 12 and so the probability is $\frac{1}{36}$.

If the question concerned more than two dice there would be a very large number of equally likely outcomes and this method would be impractical. An alternative method is to regard throwing a 6 with the first die as event *A* and throwing a 6 with the second die as event *B*. Now use the law that the probability of two independent events both happening is the product of their separate probabilities.

2

If *A* and *B* are independent events P(*A* and *B*) = P(*A*)P(*B*).

> P(A and B) is the probability of events A and B both happening.

The probability of obtaining a total score of 12 (which can only be achieved by throwing a six with both dice) is
$\frac{1}{6} \times \frac{1}{6} = \frac{1}{36}$, as before.

> The law can be extended to three or more independent events.

EXERCISE 2C

1 The probability of Brian passing a driving test is 0.6. The probability of Syra passing an advanced motoring test is 0.7. Find the probability of Brian passing a driving test and Syra passing an advanced motoring test.

2 The probability of a TV set requiring repair within 1 year is 0.22. The probability of a washing machine requiring repair within a year is 0.10. Find the probability of a TV set and a washing machine both requiring repair within a year.

3 Two coins are tossed. Find the probability of them both falling heads.

4 The probability that a vinegar bottle filled by a machine contains less than the nominal quantity is 0.1. Find the probability that two bottles, selected at random both contain:

(a) less than the nominal quantity,

(b) at least the nominal quantity.

5 Three coins are tossed. Find the probability of them all falling tails.

If you wish to find the probability of a total score of 4 when two dice are thrown then you can observe that there are three

outcomes which give a total score of 4 and the probability is $\frac{3}{36}$.

```
1,1    1,2    1,3    1,4    1,5    1,6
2,1    2,2    2,3    2,4    2,5    2,6
3,1    3,2    3,3    3,4    3,5    3,6
4,1    4,2    4,3    4,4    4,5    4,6
5,1    5,2    5,3    5,4    5,5    5,6
6,1    6,2    6,3    6,4    6,5    6,6
```

Alternatively you can answer the question using the laws of probability.

There are three outcomes which give a total score of 4:

1,3 with probability $\frac{1}{6} \times \frac{1}{6} = \frac{1}{36}$;

2,2 with probability $\frac{1}{6} \times \frac{1}{6} = \frac{1}{36}$;

3,1 with probability $\frac{1}{6} \times \frac{1}{6} = \frac{1}{36}$.

Since these three outcomes are mutually exclusive you can apply the addition law of probability and obtain the probability of

obtaining a total score of 4 as $\frac{1}{36} + \frac{1}{36} + \frac{1}{36} = \frac{3}{36} = \frac{1}{12}$.

Worked example 2.3

The probability that telephone calls to a railway timetable enquiry service are answered is 0.7. If three calls are made find the probability that:

(a) all three are answered,

(b) exactly two are answered.

Solution

If A is the event of a call being answered, $P(A) = 0.7$.

A' is the probability of a call not being answered and $P(A') = 1 - 0.7 = 0.3$.

(a) Using the multiplication law the probability of $AAA = 0.7 \times 0.7 \times 0.7 = 0.343$.

> The law for three independent events is used.

(b) If one call is unanswered it could be the first, second or third call.

$A'AA$ with probability $0.3 \times 0.7 \times 0.7 = 0.147$
$AA'A$ with probability $0.7 \times 0.3 \times 0.7 = 0.147$
AAA' with probability $0.7 \times 0.7 \times 0.3 = 0.147$

These three outcomes are mutually exclusive and so you can apply the addition law and find the probability of exactly two calls being answered to be

$0.147 + 0.147 + 0.147 = 0.441$.

> Although A' occurs in different positions the probability of each of the three outcomes is the same.

2.6 Tree diagrams

An alternative approach to the problem is to illustrate the outcomes with a tree diagram. Each branch shows the possible outcomes of each call and their probabilities. The outcome of the three calls is found by reading along the branches leading to it and the probability of this outcome is found by multiplying the individual probabilities along these branches.

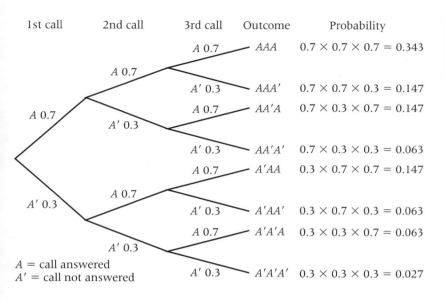

Note the sum of all the probabilities is 1. This is because one of the outcomes must occur.

2

A = call answered
A' = call not answered

The probability of all three calls being answered (AAA) can be seen to be 0.343.

The probability of exactly two calls being answered is the sum of the probabilities of the three outcomes AAA', $AA'A$ and $A'AA = 0.147 + 0.147 + 0.147 = 0.441$ as before.

Worked example 2.4

A coin is tossed three times. Find the probability that the number of tails is 0, 1, 2 or 3.

Solution

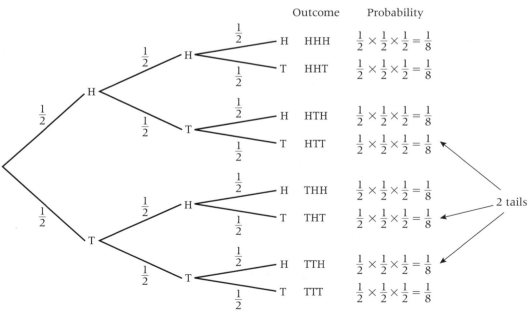

The probability of 0 tails is $\frac{1}{8}$;

The probability of 1 tail is $\frac{1}{8} + \frac{1}{8} + \frac{1}{8} = \frac{3}{8}$;

The probability of 2 tails is $\frac{1}{8} + \frac{1}{8} + \frac{1}{8} = \frac{3}{8}$;

The probability of 3 tails is $\frac{1}{8}$.

EXERCISE 2D

Answer the following questions using tree diagrams or the laws of probability.

1 The probability of Michelle passing a mathematics exam is 0.3 and the probability of her passing a biology exam is independently 0.45.

Find the probability that she:

(a) passes mathematics and fails biology,

(b) passes exactly one of the two examinations,

(c) passes at least one of the two examinations.

2 A civil servant is given the task of calculating pension entitlements. For any given calculation the probability of the result being incorrect is 0.08.

(a) Find the probability that if two pension entitlements are calculated the number incorrect will be:

(i) 0, **(ii)** 1, **(iii)** at least 1.

(b) Find the probability that if three pension entitlements are calculated the number incorrect will be:

(i) 0, **(ii)** 1, **(iii)** 2 or more.

3 The probability of answering a multiple choice question correctly by guessing is 0.25.

(a) A student guesses the answer to two multiple choice questions. Find the probability that:

(i) both answers are correct,

(ii) exactly one answer is correct.

(b) Another student guesses the answer to three multiple choice questions. Find the probability that:

(i) no answers are correct,

(ii) exactly two answers are correct,

(iii) at least two answers are correct,

(iv) less than two answers are correct.

(c) If the second student guesses the answer to four multiple choice questions find the probability that no answers are correct.

4 An opinion poll is to investigate whether estate agents'
earnings are thought to be too high, about right or too low.
The probabilities of answers from randomly selected adults
are as follows:

Too high	0.80
About right	0.15
Too low	0.05.

(a) Find the probability that if two adults are selected at
random they will:

   (i) both answer 'too high',

   (ii) one answer 'too high' and one answer 'about right',

   (iii) both give the same answer,

   (iv) neither answer 'too low',

   (v) both give different answers.

(b) Find the probability that if three adults are selected at
random they will:

   (i) all answer 'too high',

   (ii) two answer 'too high' and one answers 'about right',

   (iii) none answer 'too high',

   (iv) all give the same answer,

   (v) all give different answers.

2.7 Conditional probability

A room contains 25 people. The table shows the numbers of
each sex and whether or not they were wearing glasses.

	Male	Female
Glasses	4	5
No glasses	5	11

A person is selected at random.

F is the event that the person selected is female.

G is the event that the person selected is wearing glasses.

There are a total of nine people wearing glasses so $P(G) = \dfrac{9}{25}$.

However, only four of the nine males are wearing glasses and so
for the males the probability of wearing glasses is $\dfrac{4}{9}$ while for
the females the probability is $\dfrac{5}{16}$. That is, the probability of event
G occurring is affected by whether or not event F has occurred.
The two events are **not independent**.

The **conditional probability** that the person selected is wearing glasses given that they are female is denoted **P(G|F)**.

P(A|B) denotes the probability that event A happens given that event B happens.

Two events A and B are independent if P(A) = P(A|B).

Worked example 2.5

Students on the first year of a science course at a university take an optional language module. The number of students of each sex choosing each available language is shown below.

	French	German	Russian	Total
Male	17	9	14	40
Female	12	11	7	30
Total	29	20	21	70

A student is selected at random.

M is the event that the student selected is male.

R is the event that the student selected is studying Russian.

Write down the value of:

(a) P(M), **(b)** P(R), **(c)** P(M|R), **(d)** P(M and R), **(e)** P(M or R),
(f) P(R|M), **(g)** P(M′), **(h)** P(R′), **(i)** P(R|M′), **(j)** P(R′|M),
(k) P(M′ and R), **(l)** P(M or R′).

Solution

(a) There are 40 male students out of a total of 70

$$P(M) = \frac{40}{70} = 0.571.$$

(b) 21 students are studying Russian. $P(R) = \frac{21}{70} = 0.3$.

(c) There are 21 students studying Russian of whom 14 are male. $P(M|R) = \frac{14}{21} = 0.667$.

(d) There are 14 students who are both male and studying Russian. $P(M \text{ and } R) = \frac{14}{70} = 0.2$.

(e) There are $17 + 9 + 14 + 7 = 47$ students who are either male or studying Russian (or both). $P(M \text{ or } R) = \frac{47}{70} = 0.671$.

(f) There are 40 male students of whom 14 are studying Russian. $P(R|M) = 14/40 = 0.35$.

(g) There are 30 students who are not male (i.e. are female).
$$P(M') = \frac{30}{70} = 0.429.$$

(h) There are $17 + 9 + 12 + 11 = 49$ students who are not studying Russian. $P(R') = \frac{49}{70} = 0.7$.

(i) Of the 30 not male (female) students seven are studying Russian. $P(R|M') = \frac{7}{30} = 0.233$.

(j) Of the 40 male students $17 + 9 = 26$ are not studying Russian. $P(R'|M) = \frac{26}{40} = 0.65$.

(k) There are seven students who are not male (female) and are studying Russian. $P(M' \text{ and } R) = \frac{7}{70} = 0.1$.

(l) There are $17 + 9 + 14 + 12 + 11 = 63$ students who are either male or not studying Russian (or both).
$$P(M \text{ or } R') = \frac{63}{70} = 0.9.$$

EXERCISE 2E

1 One hundred and twenty students register for a foundation course. At the end of a year they are recorded as pass or fail. A summary of the results, classified by age, is shown.

	Age (years)	
	Under 20	**20 and over**
Pass	47	33
Fail	28	12

A student is selected at random from the list of those who registered for the course.

Q denotes the event that the selected student is under 20.

R denotes the event that the selected student passed.

(Q' and R' denote the events 'not Q' and 'not R', respectively).

Determine the value of:

(a) $P(Q)$, **(b)** $P(R)$, **(c)** $P(Q')$, **(d)** $P(Q \text{ and } R)$, **(e)** $P(Q \text{ or } R)$,
(f) $P(Q|R)$, **(g)** $P(R'|Q)$, **(h)** $P(Q|R')$, **(i)** $P(Q'|R)$,
(j) $P(Q \text{ and } R')$.

2 Last year the employees of a firm either received no pay rise, a small pay rise or a large pay rise. The following table shows the number in each category, classified by whether they were weekly paid or monthly paid.

	No pay rise	Small pay rise	Large pay rise
Weekly paid	25	85	5
Monthly paid	4	8	23

A tax inspector decides to investigate the tax affairs of an employee selected at random.

D is the event that a weekly paid employee is selected.

E is the event that an employee who received no pay rise is selected.

D' and E' are the events 'not D' and 'not E', respectively.

Find:

(a) $P(D)$, **(b)** $P(E')$, **(c)** $P(D|E)$, **(d)** $P(D$ or $E)$, **(e)** $P(E$ and $D)$,

(f) $P(D$ and $E')$, **(g)** $P(E$ or $D')$, **(h)** $P(D|E')$, **(i)** $P(E'|D')$.

3 A car hire firm has depots in Falmouth and Tiverton. The cars are classified small, medium and large according to their engine size. The number of cars in each class, based at each depot, is shown in the following table.

	Small	Medium	Large
Falmouth	12	15	13
Tiverton	18	22	10

One of the 90 cars is selected at random for inspection.

A is the event that the selected car is based at Falmouth.

B is the event that the selected car is small.

C is the event that the selected car is large.

A', B' and C' are the events 'not A', 'not B' and 'not C', respectively.

Evaluate:

(a) $P(A)$, **(b)** $P(B')$, **(c)** $P(A$ or $C)$, **(d)** $P(A$ and $B)$,

(e) $P(A$ or $B')$, **(f)** $P(A|C)$, **(g)** $P(C|A')$, **(h)** $P(B'|A)$,

(i) $P(B$ and $C)$.

By comparing your answers to **(a)** and **(f)** state whether or not the events A and C are independent.

Multiplication law

You have seen that if A and B are independent events
$P(A \text{ and } B) = P(A)P(B)$. This is a special case of the more general law that

 $P(A \text{ and } B) = P(A)P(B|A)$

A and B may consist of different outcomes of the same trial or of outcomes of different trials.

2

You can verify this using the earlier example:

	Male	Female
Glasses	4	5
No glasses	5	11

A person is selected at random.
F is the event that the person selected is female.
G is the event that the person selected is wearing glasses.

Here *F* and *G* consist of different outcomes of the same trial.

$P(F \text{ and } G)$, the probability that the person selected is a female wearing glasses is $\frac{5}{25}$ or 0.2.

$P(F) = \frac{16}{25}$

$P(G|F)$, the probability that the person selected is wearing glasses given that they are female, is $\frac{5}{16}$.

$P(F)P(G|F) = \frac{16}{25} \times \frac{5}{16} = 0.2 = P(F \text{ and } G)$

Worked example 2.6

Sheena buys ten apparently identical oranges. Unknown to her the flesh of two of these oranges is rotten. She selects two of the ten oranges at random and gives them to her grandson. Find the probability that:

(a) both the oranges are rotten,

(b) exactly one of the oranges is rotten.

Solution

(a) P(1st rotten and 2nd rotten)
   = P(1st rotten) × P(2nd rotten | 1st rotten)

   $P(\text{1st rotten}) = \frac{2}{10}$

   There are now only nine oranges left to choose from, of which one is rotten.

   $P(\text{2nd rotten} | \text{1st rotten}) = \frac{1}{9}$

   The probability that both oranges are rotten is

   $\frac{2}{10} \times \frac{1}{9} = \frac{1}{45} = 0.0222.$

(b) There are two outcomes which result in one rotten orange.

1st rotten 2nd OK with probability $\dfrac{2}{10} \times \dfrac{8}{9} = \dfrac{16}{90}$

or 1st OK 2nd rotten with probability $\dfrac{8}{10} \times \dfrac{2}{9} = \dfrac{16}{90}$.

> Note that although the oranges are selected in a different order the probabilities are the same.

Since these outcomes are **mutually exclusive** we may add their probabilities to obtain the probability of exactly one rotten orange $= \dfrac{16}{90} + \dfrac{16}{90} = \dfrac{32}{90} = 0.356$.

You may prefer to solve examples like this using tree diagrams.

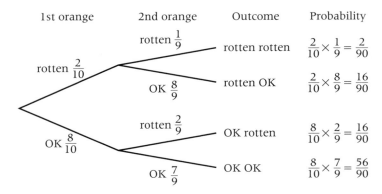

(a) The probability of both oranges being rotten is $\dfrac{2}{90} = 0.0222$.

(b) The probability of exactly one orange being rotten is $\dfrac{16}{90} + \dfrac{16}{90} = 0.356$.

Worked example 2.7

When Bali is on holiday she intends to go for a five-mile run before breakfast each day. However, sometimes she stays in bed instead. The probability that she will go for a run on the first morning is 0.7. Thereafter, the probability that she will go for a run is 0.7 if she went for a run on the previous morning and 0.6 if she did not.

Find the probability that on the first three days of the holiday she will go for:

(a) three runs,

(b) exactly two runs. [A]

Solution

(a) Probability Bali goes for three runs (RRR).

P(R 1st morning) $\times$ P(R 2nd morning$|R$ 1st morning) $\times$ P(R 3rd morning$|R$ 2nd morning) $= 0.7 \times 0.7 \times 0.7 = 0.343$.

(b) Probability that Bali runs the first two mornings and stays in bed (B) on the third morning is

P(R 1st morning) $\times$ P(R 2nd morning $|R$ 1st morning) $\times$
P(B 3rd morning $|R$ 2nd morning) $= 0.7 \times 0.7 \times 0.3 = 0.147$.

There are two other possibilities

      RBR with probability $0.7 \times 0.3 \times 0.6 = 0.126$

and

      BRR with probability $0.3 \times 0.6 \times 0.7 = 0.126$

These outcomes are mutually exclusive and so the probability of Bali going for exactly two runs is

    $0.147 + 0.126 + 0.126 = 0.399$.

EXERCISE 2F

1 A car hire firm owns 90 cars, 40 of which are based at Falmouth and the other 50 at Tiverton. If two of the 90 cars are selected at random (without replacement) find the probability that:

(a) both are based at Falmouth,

(b) one is based at Falmouth and the other at Tiverton.

2 Eight students share a house. Five of them own bicycles and three do not. If two of the students are chosen at random, to complete a survey on public transport, find the probability that:

(a) both own bicycles,

(b) one owns a bicycle and the other does not.

3 A small firm employs two sales representatives, six administrative staff and four others.

(a) If two of the 12 staff are selected at random find the probability that they are:

    (i) both sales representatives,

    (ii) one administrator and one sales representative,

    (iii) neither administrative staff.

(b) If three of the 12 staff are selected at random without replacement find the probability that they:

    (i) are all administrative staff,

    (ii) include two administrative staff and one sales representative,

    (iii) include exactly one sales representative,

    (iv) include one sales representative, one administrator and one other.

2

4 At a Cornish seaside resort, the local council displays warning flags if conditions are considered to be dangerous for bathing in the sea. The probability that flags are displayed on a particular day is 0.4 if they were displayed on the previous day, and 0.15 if they were not displayed on the previous day.

A family arrives for a three-day holiday. Assume the probability that flags are displayed on their first day is 0.3.

Determine the probability that flags are displayed on:

(a) all three days,

(b) none of the three days,

(c) exactly one of the three days. [A]

5 The probability of rain interrupting play at a county cricket ground is estimated to be 0.7 if it has interrupted play on the previous day, and 0.2 if it has not interrupted play on the previous day.

A three-day match is scheduled to start on Wednesday. The weather forecast suggests that the probability of rain interrupting play on the first day is 0.4.

Find the probability that rain will interrupt play on:

(a) Wednesday, Thursday and Friday,

(b) Wednesday and Friday, but not Thursday,

(c) Thursday and Friday only,

(d) Friday only,

(e) exactly one of the first two days (regardless of what happens on Friday),

(f) exactly one of the three days,

(g) exactly two of the three days.

6 During an epidemic a doctor is consulted by 40 people who claim to be suffering from flu. Of the 40, 15 are female of whom ten have flu and five do not. Fifteen of the males have flu and the rest do not. If three of the people are selected at random, without replacement, find the probability that:

(a) all three are female,

(b) all three have flu,

(c) all three are females with flu,

(d) all three are of the same sex,

(e) one is a female with flu and the other two are females without flu,

(f) one is male and two are female,

(g) one is a male with flu, one is a male without flu and one is a female with flu.

MIXED EXERCISE

1 A group of three pregnant women attend antenatal classes together. Assuming that each woman is equally likely to give birth on each of the seven days in a week, find the probability that all three give birth:

   (a) on a Monday,

   (b) on the same day of the week,

   (c) on different days of the week,

   (d) at a weekend (either a Saturday or Sunday).

   (e) How large would the group need to be to make the probability of all the women in the group giving birth on different days of the week less than 0.05? [A]

2 Conveyor belting for use in a chemical works is tested for strength.

   Of the pieces of belting tested at a testing station, 60% come from supplier *A* and 40% come from supplier *B*. Past experience shows that the probability of passing the strength test is 0.96 for belting from supplier *A* and 0.89 for belting from supplier *B*.

   (a) Find the probability that a randomly selected piece of belting:

   (i) comes from supplier *A* and passes the strength test,

   (ii) passes the strength test.

   The belting is also tested for safety (this test is based on the amount of heat generated if the belt snaps).

   The probability of a piece of belting from supplier A passing the safety test is 0.95 and is independent of the result of the strength test.

   (b) Find the probability that a piece of belting from supplier *A* will pass both the strength and safety tests. [A]

3 Vehicles approaching a crossroad must go in one of three directions – left, right or straight on. Observations by traffic engineers showed that of vehicles approaching from the north, 45% turn left, 20% turn right and 35% go straight on. Assuming that the driver of each vehicle chooses direction independently, what is the probability that of the next three vehicles approaching from the north:

   (a) all go straight on,

   (b) all go in the same direction,

   (c) two turn left and one turns right,

   (d) all go in different directions,

   (e) exactly two turn left? [A]

4 A bicycle shop stocks racing, touring and mountain bicycles. The following table shows the number of bicycles of each type in stock, together with their price range.

	Price range		
	< £250	**£250–£500**	**> £500**
Racing	10	18	22
Touring	36	22	12
Mountain	28	32	20

A bicycle is selected at random for testing.

R is the event that a racing bicycle is selected.

S is the event that a bicycle worth between £250 and £500 is selected.

T is the event that a touring bicycle is selected.

(*R'*, *S'*, *T'* are the events 'not *R*', 'not *S*', 'not *T*', respectively.)

(a) Write down the value of:

    (i) P(*S*),   **(ii)** P(*R* and *S*),

    (iii) P(*T'* or *S'*)   **(iv)** P(*S* | *R*).

(b) Express in terms of the events that have been defined the event that a mountain bicycle is selected.   [A]

5 The probability that telephone calls to a railway timetable enquiry service are answered is 0.7.

(a) If three calls are made, find the probability that:

    (i) all three are answered,

    (ii) exactly two are answered.

(b) Ahmed requires some timetable information and decides that if his call is not answered he will call repeatedly until he obtains an answer.

Find the probability that to obtain an answer he has to call:

    (i) exactly three times,

    (ii) at least three times.

(c) If a call is answered, the probability that the information given is correct is 0.8. Thus, there are three possible outcomes for each call:

    call not answered

    call answered but incorrect information given

    call answered and correct information given.

If three calls are made, find the probability that each outcome occurs once.   [A]

2

6 At the beginning of 1992 a motor insurance company classified its customers as low, medium or high risk. The following table shows the number of customers in each category and whether or not they made a claim during 1992.

	Low	Medium	High
No claim in 1992	4200	5100	3900
Claim in 1992	200	500	1100

(a) A customer is selected at random.

A is the event that the customer made a claim in 1992.

B is the event that the customer was classified low risk.

A' is the event 'not A'.

Write down the value of:

(i) $P(A)$

(ii) $P(A|B)$

(iii) $P(B|A')$

(iv) $P(A \text{ and } B)$

(v) $P(B \text{ or } A')$.

(b) As a result of the data in **(a)** the company decided not to accept any new high risk customers (but existing customers could continue). In June 1993 its customers were 30% low risk, 65% medium risk and 5% high risk. Use the data in the table above to estimate, for each category of customer, the probability of a claim being made in the next year. Hence estimate the probability that a randomly selected customer will make a claim in the next year. [A]

7 A market researcher wishes to interview residents aged 18 years and over in a small village. The adult population of the village is made up as follows.

Age group	Male	Female
18–29	16	24
30–59	29	21
60 and over	15	25

(a) When one person is selected at random for interview:

A is the event of the person selected being male.

B is the event of the person selected being in the age group 30–59.

C is the event of the person selected being aged 60 or over.

(A', B', C' are the events 'not A', 'not B' and 'not C', respectively.)

Write down the value of

(i) P(*A*)

(ii) P(*A* and *B*)

(iii) P(*A* or *C'*)

(iv) P(*B'* | *A*).

(b) When three people are selected for interview, what is the probability that they are all female if:

    (i) one is selected at random from each age group,

    (ii) they are selected at random, without replacement, from the population of 130 people?

Three people are selected at random, without replacement.

(c) What is the probability that there will be one from each of the three age groups? [A]

Key point summary

I Probability is measured on a scale from 0 to 1.   *p13*

2 If a trial can result in one of *n* equally likely   *p14* outcomes and an event consists of *r* of these, then the probability of the event happening as a result of the trial is $\frac{r}{n}$.

3 Two events are **mutually exclusive** if they cannot   *p16* both happen.

4 If *A* and *B* are **mutually exclusive** events   *p16* P(*A* or *B*) = P(*A*) + P(*B*).

5 The event of *A* not happening as the result of a trial   *p17* is called the **complement** of *A* and is usually denoted *A'*.

6 Two events are **independent** if the probability of   *p18* one happening is unaffected by whether or not the other happens.

7 If *A* and *B* are **independent** events   *p19* P(*A* and *B*) = P(*A*)P(*B*).

8 P(*A* | *B*) denotes the probability that event *A* happens *p24* given that event *B* happens.

9 If events *A* and *B* are **independent** P(*A* | *B*) = P(*A*).   *p24*

10 P(*A* and *B*) = P(*A*)P(*B* | *A*) = P(*B*)P(*A* | *B*).   *p27*

2

Test yourself	What to review
1 Twelve components include three that are defective. If two components are chosen at random from the 12 find the probability that: **(a)** both are defective, **(b)** exactly one is defective.	*Section 2.7*
2 Under what conditions does P(R and Q) = P(R)P(Q)?	*Section 2.5*
3 Under what conditions does P(S or T) = P(S) + P(T)?	*Section 2.4*
4 A student is selected from a class. R is the event that the student is female. Describe the complement of R. How is the complement usually denoted?	*Section 2.4*
5 There are 15 male and 20 female passengers on a tram. Ten of the males and 16 of the females are aged over 25. A ticket inspector selects one of the passengers at random. A is the event that the person selected is female, B is the event that the person selected is over 25. Write down P(A), P(B), P(A | B), P(A and B) and P(A or B). Hence verify that P(A and B) = P(B)P(A | B). Why is it not possible to apply the law P(A or B) = P(A) + P(B) in this case?	*Section 2.7*
6 It is estimated that the probability of a league cricket match ending in a home win is 0.4, an away win is 0.25 and a draw is 0.35. Find the probability that if three games are played, and the results are independent, there will be: **(a)** three home wins, **(b)** exactly one home win, **(c)** one home win, one away win and one draw.	*Sections 2.5 and 2.6*

Test yourself ANSWERS

6 (a) 0.064; **(b)** 0.432; **(c)** 0.21.

5 $\frac{4}{7}, \frac{26}{35}, \frac{8}{13}, \frac{16}{35}, \frac{6}{7}$; P(B) × P(A \| B) = $\frac{26}{35} × \frac{8}{13} = \frac{16}{35}$ = P(A and B),

A and B are not mutually exclusive.

4 Student is male, R'.

3 S and T mutually exclusive events.

2 R and Q independent events.

1 (a) 0.0455; **(b)** 0.409.

The normal distribution

Learning objectives

After studying this chapter, you should be able to:
- use tables to find probabilities from any normal distribution
- use tables of percentage points of the normal distribution
- understand what is meant by the distribution of the sample mean
- find probabilities involving sample means.

3.1 Continuous distributions

For continuous variables such as height, weight or distance it is not possible to list all the possible outcomes. In this case probability is represented by the area under a curve (called the probability density function).

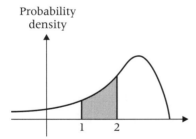

The probability that an observation, selected at random from the distribution, lies between 1 and 2 is represented by the shaded area. Note that the probability that an observation from a continuous distribution is exactly equal to 2 (or any other value) is zero.

There are two conditions for a curve to be used as a probability density function:

- the total area under the curve must be 1

- the curve must not take negative values, that is, it must not go below the horizontal axis.

3.2 The normal distribution

Many continuous variables, which occur naturally, have a probability density function like this.

This is called a normal distribution. It has a high probability density close to the mean and this decreases as you move away from the mean.

> The main features of normal distribution are that it is:
> - bell shaped
> - symmetrical (about the mean)
> - the total area under the curve is 1 (as with all probability density functions).

Examples of variables which are likely to follow a normal distribution are the heights of adult females in the United Kingdom, the lengths of leaves from oak trees, the widths of car doors coming off a production line and the times taken by 12-year-old boys to run 100 m.

3.3 The standard normal distribution

Normal distributions may have any mean and any standard deviation. The normal distribution with mean 0 and standard deviation 1 is called the **standard normal distribution**.

> The equation of the probability density function (p.d.f.) is
>
> $$\frac{1}{\sqrt{2\pi}} e^{-\frac{z^2}{2}}$$

Z is, by convention, used to denote a standard normal variable.

Finding areas under this curve would involve some very difficult integration. Fortunately this has been done for you and the results tabulated. The tables are in the Appendix and an extract is shown in the next section.

3.4 The normal distribution function

The table gives the probability, p, that a normally distributed random variable Z, with mean $= 0$ and variance $= 1$, is less than or equal to z.

0.06 column

z	0.00	0.01	0.02	0.03	0.04	0.05	0.06	0.07	0.08	0.09	
1.2	0.88493	0.88688	0.88877	0.89065	0.89251	0.89435	0.89617	0.89796	0.89973	0.90147	1.2
1.3	0.90320	0.90490	0.90658	0.90824	0.90988	0.91149	0.91309	0.91466	0.91621	0.91774	1.3
1.4	0.91924	0.92073	0.92220	0.92364	0.92507	0.92647	0.92785	0.92922	0.93056	0.93189	1.4
1.5	0.93319	0.93448	0.93574	0.93699	0.93822	0.93943	0.94062	0.94179	0.94295	0.94408	1.5
1.6	0.94520	0.94630	0.94738	0.94845	0.94950	0.95053	0.95154	0.95254	0.95352	0.95449	1.6

1.3 row →

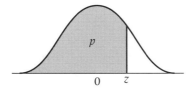

As the diagram above shows, the area to the left of a particular value of z is tabulated. This represents the probability, p, that an observation, selected at random from a standard normal distribution (i.e. mean 0, standard deviation 1), will be less than z.

> The probability of an observation $< z$ is the same as the probability of an observation $\leq z$.

To use these tables for a positive values of z, say **1.36**, take the digits before and after the decimal point and locate the appropriate row of the table. In this case the row, where z is **1.3** (see diagram in the margin). Then look along this row to find the probability in the column headed **0.06**. This gives 0.913 09 meaning that the probability that an observation from a standard normal distribution is less than 1.36 is 0.913 09.

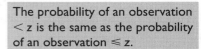

If the z-value is given to more than two decimal places, say 0.468, the appropriate value of p will lie between 0.677 24 (the value for $z = 0.46$) and 0.680 82 (the value for $z = 0.47$). An exact value could be estimated using interpolation. However, it is easier and perfectly acceptable to round the z to 0.47 and then use the tables.

> We will never need a final answer correct to five significant figures but if this is an intermediate stage of a calculation as many figures as possible should be kept.

EXERCISE 3A

Find the probability that an observation from a standard normal distribution will be less than:

(a) 1.23, **(b)** 0.97, **(c)** 1.85, **(d)** 0.42, **(e)** 0.09,

(f) 1.57, **(g)** 1.94, **(h)** 0.603, **(i)** 2.358, **(j)** 1.053 79.

Probability greater than z

If we wish to find the probability of a value greater than 1.36 this is represented by the area to the right of 1.36. We need to use the fact that the total area under the curve is 1.

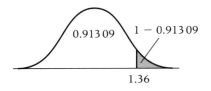

In this case $P(z > 1.36) = 1 - 0.913\,09 = 0.0869$.

EXERCISE 3B

1 Find the probability that an observation from a standard normal distribution will be greater than:

(**a**) 1.36,   (**b**) 0.58,   (**c**) 1.23,   (**d**) 0.86,

(**e**) 0.32,   (**f**) 1.94,   (**g**) 2.37,   (**h**) 0.652,

(**i**) 0.087,   (**j**) 1.3486.

Negative values of z

Negative values of z are not included in the tables. This is because we can use the fact that the normal distribution is symmetrical to derive them from the positive values.

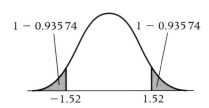

For example, $P(z < -1.52) = P(z > 1.52)$

$$P(z < -1.52) = 1 - 0.935\,74 = 0.064\,26$$

Similarly, $P(z > -0.59) = P(z < 0.59) = 0.722\,40$.

EXERCISE 3C

1 Find the probability that an observation from a standard normal distribution will be:

(**a**) less than -1.39,

(**b**) less than -0.58,

(**c**) more than -1.09,

(**d**) more than -0.47,

(**e**) less than or equal to -0.45,

(**f**) greater than or equal to -0.32,

(**g**) less than -0.64,

(**h**) -0.851 or greater,

(**i**) more than -0.747,

(**j**) less than -0.4398.

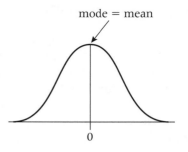

3.5 Probability between *z*-values

To find the probability that *z* lies between two values we may have to use both symmetry and the fact that the total area under the curve is 1. It is essential to draw a diagram. Remember that the mean of a standard normal distribution is 0 and so positive values are to the right of the mode and negative values to the left. The following three examples cover the different possibilities.

3

- $P(0.6 < z < 1.2)$

  We require:

  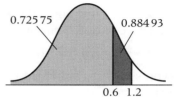

  > (area to left of 1.2) − (area to left of 0.6)
  > $= 0.884\,93 - 0.725\,75$
  > $= 0.159$

- $P(-2.1 < z < -1.7)$

  Here the *z*-values are negative, and so although we could still use areas to the left of *z* it is easier to use:

  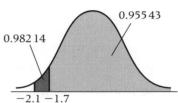

  > (area right of −2.1) − (area right of −1.7)
  > $= 0.982\,14 - 0.955\,43$
  > $= 0.0267$

- $P(-0.8 < z < 1.4)$

  We require:

  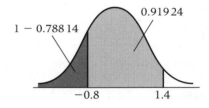

  > (area left of 1.4) − (area left of −0.8)
  > $= 0.919\,24 - (1 - 0.788\,14)$
  > $= 0.707$

EXERCISE 3D

1 Find the probability that an observation from a standard normal distribution will be between:

(a) 0.2 and 0.8,

(b) −1.25 and −0.84,

(c) −0.7 and 0.7,

(d) −1.2 and 2.4,

(e) 0.76 and 1.22,

(f) −3 and −2,

(g) −1.27 and 2.33,

(h) 0.44 and 0.45,

(i) −1.2379 and −0.8888,

(j) −2.3476 and 1.9987.

3.6 Standardising a normal variable

The wingspans of a population of birds are normally distributed with mean 14.1 cm and standard deviation 1.7 cm. We may be asked to calculate the probability that a randomly selected bird has a wingspan less than 17.0 cm. Tables of the normal distribution with mean 14.1 and standard deviation 1.7 do not exist. However, we can use tables of the standard normal distribution by first standardising the value of interest. That is, we express it as standard deviations from the mean.

For example, for a normal distribution with mean 50 cm and standard deviation 5 cm, a value of 60 cm is:

$60 - 50 = 10$ cm from the mean.

To express this as standard deviations from the mean we divide by 5 cm.

$$\frac{10}{5} = 2$$

This is the standardised or z-score of 60 cm.

> For a value, x, from a normal distribution with mean μ and standard deviation σ,
>
> $$z = \frac{x - \mu}{\sigma}$$

For the distribution with mean 50 cm, standard deviation 5 cm the z-score of 47 cm is $\dfrac{(47 - 50)}{5} = -0.6$. Note the importance of the sign which tells us whether the value is to the left or the right of the mean.

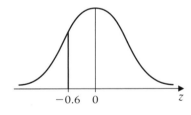

EXERCISE 3E

1 A normal distribution has mean 40 cm and standard deviation 5 cm. Find the standardised values of:

(a) 47 cm,   (b) 43 cm,   (c) 36 cm,   (d) 32 cm,

(e) 50.5 cm.

2 A normal distribution has mean 36.3 s and standard deviation 4.6 s. Find the z-scores of:

(a) 39.3 s,   (b) 30.0 s,   (c) 42.5 s,   (d) 28.0 s.

3 The wingspans of a population of birds are approximately normally distributed with mean 18.1 cm and standard deviation 1.8 cm. Find standardised values of:

(a) 20.2 cm,   (b) 17.8 cm,   (c) 19.3 cm,   (d) 16.0 cm.

3.7 Probabilities from a normal distribution

We said at the beginning of the previous section that you might want to find the probability that a bird randomly selected from a population with mean wingspan 14.1 cm and standard deviation 1.7 cm would have a wingspan less than 17 cm. We can now do this. First calculate the z-score:

$$z = \frac{(17 - 14.1)}{1.7} = 1.71$$

Now enter the tables at 1.71.

We find that the probability of a wingspan less than 17 cm is 0.956.

Some students wonder whether less than 17 cm really means less than 16.5 cm. **Don't**. Just use the value given. Otherwise you would also have to say that the standard deviation is between 1.65 and 1.75 cm and the calculation becomes impossible to carry out.

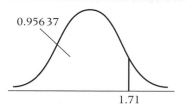

Worked example 3.1

The chest measurements of adult male customers for T-shirts may be modelled by a normal distribution with mean 101 cm and standard deviation 5 cm. Find the probability that a randomly selected customer will have a chest measurement which is:

(a) less than 103 cm,

(b) 98 cm or more,

(c) between 95 cm and 100 cm,

(d) between 90 cm and 110 cm.

Solution

(a) $z = \frac{(103 - 101)}{5} = 0.4$,

probability less than 103 cm is 0.655;

(b) $z = \frac{(98 - 101)}{5} = -0.6$,

probability 98 cm or more is 0.726;

(c) $z_1 = \frac{(95 - 101)}{5} = -1.2$,

$z_2 = \frac{(100 - 101)}{5} = -0.2$,

probability between 95 cm and 100 cm is
0.884 93 − 0.579 26 = 0.306;

(d) $z_1 = \frac{(90 - 101)}{5} = -2.2$,

$z_2 = \frac{(110 - 101)}{5} = 1.8$,

probability between 90 cm and 101 cm is
0.964 07 − (1 − 0.986 10) = 0.950.

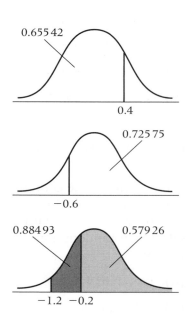

EXERCISE 3F

(In this exercise give the answers correct to three significant figures or to the accuracy found from tables if this is less than three significant figures.)

1 A variable is normally distributed with a mean of 19.6 cm and a standard deviation of 1.9 cm. Find the probability that an item chosen at random from this distribution will have a measurement:

   (a) less than 20.4 cm,

   (b) more than 22.0 cm,

   (c) 17.5 cm or less,

   (d) 22.6 cm or less,

   (e) between 19.0 and 21.0 cm,

   (f) between 20.5 cm and 22.5 cm.

2 The weights of a certain animal are approximately normally distributed with a mean of 36.4 kg and a standard deviation of 4.7 kg. Find the probability that when one of these animals is chosen at random it will have a weight:

   (a) 40.0 kg or less,

   (b) between 32.0 kg and 41.0 kg,

   (c) more than 45.0 kg,

   (d) less than 28.0 kg,

   (e) 30.0 kg or more,

   (f) between 30.0 kg and 35.0 kg.

3 The weights of the contents of jars of jam packed by a machine are approximately normally distributed with a mean of 460.0 g and a standard deviation of 14.5 g. A jar of jam is selected at random. Find the probability that its contents will weigh:

   (a) less than 450 g,

   (b) 470.0 g or less,

   (c) between 440.0 and 480.0 g,

   (d) 475 g or more,

   (e) more than 454 g,

   (f) between 450 g and 475 g.

4 The lengths of leaves from a particular plant are approximately normally distributed with a mean of 28.4 cm and a standard deviation of 2.6 cm. When a leaf is chosen at random what is the probability its length is:

(a) between 25.0 cm and 30.0 cm,

(b) more than 32.0 cm,

(c) less than 24.0 cm,

(d) 27.0 cm or more,

(e) 26.0 cm or less,

(f) between 24.0 cm and 28.0 cm?

5 The volumes of the discharges made by a drink dispensing machine into cups is approximately normally distributed with a mean of 465.0 cm³ and a standard deviation of 6.8 cm³. When the volume of the contents of a cup chosen at random from this machine is measured what is the probability that it will be:

(a) 470 cm³ or more,

(b) less than 458.0 cm³,

(c) between 455.0 cm³ and 475.0 cm³?

3.8 Percentage points of the normal distribution

This is an alternative way of tabulating the standard normal distribution. The z-score for a given probability, p, is tabulated.

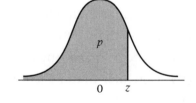

The table gives the values of z satisfying $P(Z \leq z) = p$, where Z is the normally distributed random variable with mean $= 0$ and variance $= 1$.

0.00 column →

p	0.00	0.01	0.02	0.03	0.04	0.05	0.06	0.07	0.08	0.09	
0.5	0.0000	0.0251	0.0502	0.0753	0.1004	0.1257	0.1510	0.1764	0.2019	0.2275	0.5
0.6	0.2533	0.2793	0.3055	0.3319	0.3585	0.3853	0.4125	0.4399	0.4677	0.4958	0.6
0.7	0.5244	0.5534	0.5828	0.6128	0.6433	0.6745	0.7063	0.7388	0.7722	0.8064	0.7
0.8	0.8416	0.8779	0.9154	0.9542	0.9945	1.0364	1.0803	1.1264	1.1750	1.2265	0.8
0.9	1.2816	1.3408	1.4051	1.4758	1.5548	1.6449	1.7507	1.8808	2.0537	2.3263	0.9

0.9 row →

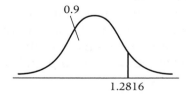

If we require the z-score which exceeds 0.9, or 90% of the normal distribution, we would locate the row **0.9** and then take the entry in the column **0.00**. This gives a z-score of 1.2816.

Values of p less than 0.5 are not tabulated. To find the z-score which exceeds 0.05, or 5% of the distribution, we need to use symmetry. The z-score will clearly be negative but will be of the same magnitude as the z-score which exceeds $1 - 0.05 = 0.95$ of the distribution. Thus, the required value is -1.6449.

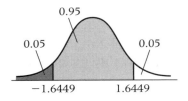

We often require to find the z-scores which are symmetrical about the mean and contain 95% of the distribution. The two tails will contain 5% in total. They will therefore contain $\frac{5}{2} = 2.5\%$ each. The upper z-score will exceed $100 - 2.5 = 97.5\%$ of the distribution. Entering the table at 0.975 we find a z-score of 1.96. The lower z-score is, by symmetry, -1.96.

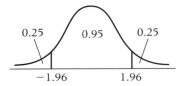

p	0.00	0.01	0.02	0.03	0.04	0.05	0.06	0.07	0.08	0.09	
0.95	1.6449	1.6546	1.6646	1.6747	1.6849	1.6954	1.7060	1.7169	1.7279	1.7392	0.95
0.96	1.7507	1.7624	1.7744	1.7866	1.7991	1.8119	1.8250	1.8384	1.8522	1.8663	0.96
0.97	1.8808	1.8957	1.9110	1.9268	1.9431	1.9600	1.9774	1.9954	2.0141	2.0335	0.97
0.98	2.0537	2.0749	2.0969	2.1201	2.1444	2.1701	2.1973	2.2252	2.2571	2.2094	0.98
0.99	2.3263	2.3656	2.4089	2.4573	2.5121	2.5758	2.6521	2.7478	2.8782	3.0902	0.99

EXERCISE 3G

1 Find the z-score which:

   (a) is greater than 97.5% of the population,

   (b) is less than 90% of the population,

   (c) exceeds 5% of the population,

   (d) is exceeded by 7.5% of the population,

   (e) is greater than 2.5% of the distribution,

   (f) is less than 15% of the population,

   (g) exceeds 20% of the distribution,

   (h) is greater than 90% of the distribution,

   (i) is less than 1% of the population.

2 Find the z-scores which are symmetrical about the mean and contain:

   (a) 90% of the distribution,

   (b) 99% of the distribution,

   (c) 99.8% of the distribution.

Applying results to normal distributions

To apply these results to normal distributions, other than the standard normal, we need to recall that z-scores are in units of standard deviations from the mean. Thus if x is normally distributed with mean μ and standard deviation σ,

$$x = \mu + z\sigma.$$

> Note that this is only a rearrangement of the formula $z = (x - \mu)/\sigma$.

Worked example 3.2

The wingspans of a population of birds are normally distributed with mean 14.1 cm and standard deviation 1.7 cm. Find:

(a) the wingspan which will exceed 90% of the population,

(b) the wingspan which will exceed 20% of the population,

(c) the limits of the central 95% of the wingspans.

Solution

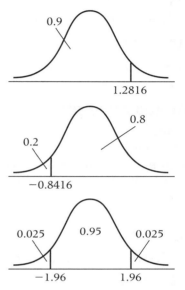

(a) The z-score which exceeds 90% of the population is 1.2816. The value required is therefore 1.2816 standard deviations above the mean, i.e.

$$14.1 + 1.2816 \times 1.7 = 16.3 \text{ cm}.$$

(b) The z-score which will exceed 20% of the population will be exceeded by 80% of the population.

$$z = -0.8416$$
$$x = 14.1 - 0.8416 \times 1.7 = 12.7 \text{ cm}.$$

(c) $z = \pm 1.96$

The central 95% of wingspans are $14.1 \pm 1.96 \times 1.7$, i.e.

$$14.1 \pm 3.33 \text{ or } 10.8 \text{ cm to } 17.4 \text{ cm}.$$

EXERCISE 3H

1 A large shoal of fish have lengths which are normally distributed with mean 74 cm and standard deviation 9 cm.

(a) What length will be exceeded by 10% of the shoal?

(b) What length will be exceeded by 25% of the shoal?

(c) What length will be exceeded by 70% of the shoal?

(d) What length will exceed 95% of the shoal?

(e) Find the limits of the central 90% of lengths.

(f) Find the limits of the central 60% of lengths.

2 Hamburger meat is sold in 1 kg packages. The fat content of the packages is found to be normally distributed with mean 355 g and standard deviation 40 g.

Find the fat content which will be exceeded by:

(a) 5% of the packages,

(b) 35% of the packages,

(c) 50% of the packages,

(d) 80% of the packages,

(e) 99.9% of the packages.

(f) Find the limits of the central 95% of the contents.

3 When Kate telephones for a taxi, the waiting time is normally distributed with mean 18 minutes and standard deviation 5 minutes. At what time should she telephone for a taxi if she wishes to have a probability of:

(a) 0.9 that it will arrive before 3.00 p.m.,

(b) 0.99 that it will arrive before 3.00 p.m.,

(c) 0.999 that it will arrive before 3.00 p.m.,

(d) 0.2 that it will arrive before 3.00 p.m.,

(e) 0.3 that it will arrive after 3.00 p.m.,

(f) 0.8 that it will arrive after 3.00 p.m.?

Worked example 3.3

A vending machine discharges soft drinks. A total of 5% of the discharges have a volume of more than 475 cm³, while 1% have a volume less than 460 cm³. The discharges may be assumed to be normally distributed. Find the mean and standard deviation of the discharges.

Solution

5% of z-scores exceed 1.6449.

Hence, if the mean is μ and the standard deviation is σ,

$$\mu + 1.6449\sigma = 475. \quad [1]$$

1% of z-scores are below -2.3263.

Hence,

$$\mu - 2.3263\sigma = 460. \quad [2]$$

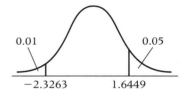

Subtracting equation [2] from equation [1] gives

$$3.9712\sigma = 15$$
$$\sigma = 3.7772$$

Substituting in equation [1]

$$\mu + 1.6449 \times 3.7772 = 475$$
$$\mu = 468.787$$

The mean is 468.79 cm³ and the standard deviation is 3.78 cm³.

Worked example 3.4

Adult male customers for T-shirts have chest measurements which may be modelled by a normal distribution with mean 101 cm and standard deviation 5 cm. T-shirts to fit customers with chest measurements less than 98 cm are classified **small**. Find the median chest measurement of customers requiring **small** T-shirts.

Solution

First find the proportion of customers requiring **small** T-shirts.

$$z = \frac{(98 - 101)}{5} = -0.6$$

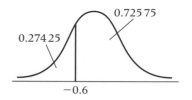

Proportion is $1 - 0.725\,75 = 0.274\,25$.

The chest measurement will be less than the median for half of these customers. That is, for,

$$\frac{0.274\,25}{2} = 0.137\,125 \text{ of all customers.}$$

The proportion of customers with chest measurements exceeding the median of those requiring small T-shirts is $1 - 0.137\,125 = 0.862\,875$.

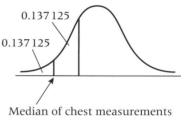

The z-score is -1.08.

Thus, the median is $101 - 1.08 \times 5 = 95.6$ cm.

Median of chest measurements of customers requiring small T-shirts

3.9 Modelling data using the normal distribution

Textbooks and examination questions often use phrases such as 'the weights of packs of butter in a supermarket may be **modelled** by a normal distribution with mean 227 g and standard deviation 7.5 g'.

The word **modelled** implies that the weights may not follow a normal distribution exactly but that calculations which assume a normal distribution will give answers which are very close to reality. For example, if you use the normal distribution to calculate the proportion of packs which weigh less than 224 g, the answer you obtain will be very close to the proportion of packs which actually weigh less than 224 g.

There are at least two reasons why the word **modelled** is used in this context:

- We could never obtain sufficient data to prove that the weights followed a particular distribution exactly without the smallest deviation in any respect.

- The theoretical normal distribution does not have any limits. That is, it would have to be theoretically possible for the packs of butter to have any weight, including negative weights, to fit a normal distribution exactly. However, this is not a practical problem since, for a normal distribution with mean μ and standard deviation σ, the central:

    68% of the area lies in the range $\mu \pm \sigma$

    95.5% of the area lies in the range $\mu \pm 2\sigma$

    99.7% of the area lies in the range $\mu \pm 3\sigma$

For example, for the packs of butter we would expect 99.7% to lie in the range

$$227 \pm 3 \times 7.5 \qquad \text{i.e. 204.5 g to 249.5 g.}$$

It would be theoretically possible to find a pack weighing 260 g which is well outside this range. However, this is so unlikely that, if we did, it would be sensible to conclude that the model was incorrect.

EXERCISE 31

1 Shoe shop staff routinely measure the length of their customers' feet. Measurements of the length of one foot (without shoes) from each of 180 adult male customers yielded a mean length of 29.2 cm and a standard deviation of 1.47 cm.

Given that the lengths of male feet may be modelled by a normal distribution, and making any other necessary assumptions, calculate an interval within which 90% of the lengths of male feet will lie.

2 Consultants employed by a large library reported that the time spent in the library by a user could be modelled by a normal distribution with mean 65 minutes and standard deviation 20 minutes.

   (a) Assuming that this model is adequate, what is the probability that a user spends:

   (i) less than 90 minutes in the library,

   (ii) between 60 and 90 minutes in the library?

The library closes at 9.00 p.m.

   (b) Explain why the model above could not apply to a user who entered the library at 8.00 p.m.

   (c) Estimate an approximate latest time of entry for which the model above could still be plausible. [A]

3 The bar receipts at a rugby club after a home league game may be modelled by a normal distribution with mean £1250 and standard deviation £210.

The club treasurer has to pay a brewery account of £1300 the day after the match.

   (a) What is the probability that she will be able to pay the whole of the account from the bar receipts?

Instead of paying the whole of the account she agrees to pay the brewery £*x*.

(b) What value of *x* would give a probability of 0.99 that the amount could be met from the bar receipts?

(c) What is the probability that the bar receipts after four home league games will all exceed £1300?

(d) Although the normal distribution may provide an adequate model for the bar receipts, give a reason why it cannot provide an exact model. [A]

3.10 Notation

Many textbooks use the notation $X \sim N(\mu, \sigma^2)$ to mean that the variable X is normally distributed with mean μ and standard deviation σ. The symbol σ^2 is the square of the standard deviation and this is called the variance.

The variance is not a natural measure of spread as it is in different units from the raw data. It does, however, have many uses in mathematical statistics. We will not use it further in this book but it does appear in later modules.

$X \sim N(27.0, 16.0)$ means that the variable X is distributed with mean 27.0 and standard deviation $\sqrt{16.0} = 4.0$.

3.11 The central limit theorem

A bakery makes loaves of bread with a mean weight of 900 g and a standard deviation of 20 g. An inspector selected four loaves at random and weighed them. It is unlikely that the mean weight of the four loaves she chose would be exactly 900 g. In fact the mean weight was 906 g. A second inspector then chose four loaves at random and found their mean weight to be 893 g. There is no limit to how many times a sample of four can be chosen and the mean weight calculated. These means will vary and will have a distribution.

This distribution is known as **the distribution of the sample mean**.

This is one of the most important statistical ideas in this book. You may not find it easy to grasp at first but you will meet it in many different contexts and this will help you to understand it.

The **central limit theorem** is a remarkable result concerning both the shape and the parameters of this distribution.

If a random sample of size n is taken from any distribution with mean μ and standard deviation σ then:

- $\bar{x}$, the sample mean, will be distributed with mean μ and standard deviation $\dfrac{\sigma}{\sqrt{n}}$,

- the distribution will be approximately normal provided n is sufficiently large – the larger the size of n the better the approximation.

This result is exact. There is no approximation.

The second part of the central limit theorem enables us to make statements about sample means without knowing the shape of the distribution they have come from. As a rule of thumb most textbooks say that the sample size, n, needs to be at least 30 to assume that the mean is normally distributed. For the purpose of examination questions it is best to stick to this figure, however it is undoubtedly on the cautious side. How large the sample needs to be depends on how much the distribution varies from the normal. For a *unimodal* distribution which is somewhat skew even samples of five or six will give a good approximation.

If the parent distribution is normal, the distribution of the sample mean is exactly normal.

If a random sample of size 50 is taken from any distribution with mean 75.2 kg and standard deviation 8.5 kg then the mean will be approximately normally distributed with mean 75.2 kg and standard deviation $\dfrac{8.5}{\sqrt{50}} = 1.20$ kg.

If the sample is of size 100 the mean will be approximately normally distributed with mean 75.2 kg and standard deviation $\dfrac{8.5}{\sqrt{100}} = 0.85$ kg.

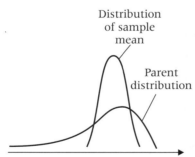

As the sample gets larger the standard deviation of the sample mean (called the **standard error**) gets smaller.

The sample means will be packed tightly around the population mean. The larger the samples become the tighter the means will be packed. This has major implications for topics which arise in other modules, including confidence intervals, hypothesis testing and quality control.

Worked example 3.5

The weights of pebbles on a beach are distributed with mean 48.6 g and standard deviation 8.5 g.

(a) A random sample of 50 pebbles is chosen. Find the probability that:

   (i) the mean weight will be less than 49.0 g,

   (ii) the mean weight will be 47.0 g or less.

(b) Find limits within which the central 95% of such sample means would lie.

(c) How large a sample would be needed in order that the central 95% of sample means would lie in an interval of width at most 4 g?

Solution

(a) The distribution of the pebble weights is unknown but since the samples are of size 50 it is safe to use the central limit theorem and assume that the sample means are approximately normally distributed. This distribution of sample means will have mean 48.6 g and standard deviation $\frac{8.5}{\sqrt{50}} = 1.2021$ g.

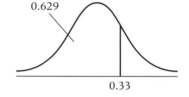

   (i) We first standardise 49.0

$$z = \frac{(49.0 - 48.6)}{(8.5/\sqrt{50})} = 0.333$$

Note for the mean of samples of size n,

$$z = \frac{(\bar{x} - \mu)}{\left(\frac{\sigma}{\sqrt{n}}\right)}$$

> Note that we have rounded 0.333 to 0.33. This is adequate but not exact. A more accurate result could be found using interpolation.

The probability that the mean is less than 49.0 g is 0.629.

   (ii) $z = \frac{(47.0 - 48.6)}{\left(\frac{8.5}{\sqrt{50}}\right)} = -1.331$

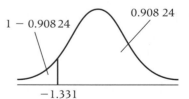

The probability that the mean will be less than 47.0 g is $1 - 0.908\,24 = 0.0918$.

(b) The central 95% of sample means will lie in the interval $\mu \pm \frac{1.96\sigma}{\sqrt{n}}$,

i.e. $48.6 \pm 1.96 \times \frac{8.5}{\sqrt{50}}$,

or 46.2 g to 51.0 g.

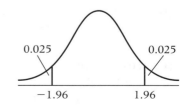

(c) As in **(b)** the central 95% of sample means will lie in the interval $\mu \pm 1.96 \dfrac{\sigma}{\sqrt{n}}$. The width of this interval is

$$\frac{3.92 \times 8.5}{\sqrt{n}}, \qquad\qquad \text{i.e.} \ \frac{33.32}{\sqrt{n}}.$$

If the interval is to be at most 4 then,

$$\frac{33.32}{\sqrt{n}} < 4$$

$$\text{i.e.} \quad \frac{33.32}{4} < \sqrt{n}$$

$$69.4 < n$$

Thus a sample of size at least 70 is needed. (Fortunately the sample size has turned out to be quite large thus justifying our earlier assumption of a normally distributed sample mean.)

EXERCISE 3J

1 A population has a mean of 57.4 kg and a standard deviation of 6.7 kg. Samples of 80 items are chosen at random from this population. Find the probability that a sample mean:

   (a) will be 58.4 g or less,

   (b) will be less than 56.3 kg,

   (c) will lie between 56.3 kg and 58.4 kg.

2 It is found that the mean of a population is 46.2 cm and its standard deviation is 2.3 cm. Samples of 100 items are chosen at random.

   (a) Between what limits would you expect the central 95% of the means from such samples to lie?

   (b) What limit would you expect to be exceeded by only 5% of the sample means?

   (c) How large should the sample size be in order for the central 95% of such sample means to lie in an interval of width at most 0.8 cm?

3 The times taken by people to complete a task are distributed with a mean of 18.0 s and a standard deviation 8.5 s. Samples of 50 times are chosen at random from this population.

(a) What is the probability that a randomly selected sample mean will:

(i) be at least 19.4 s,

(ii) be 17.5 s or more,

(iii) lie between 17.4 and 19.0 s?

(b) Between what limits would you expect the central 95% of such sample means to lie?

4 A population has a mean of 124.3 cm and a standard deviation of 14.5 cm.

(a) What size samples should be chosen in order to make the central 95% of their means lie in an interval of width as close to 5.0 cm as possible?

(b) Explain why, provided the samples are chosen at random, your answer is valid.

(c) Under what circumstances might an answer to a similar question be invalid?

MIXED EXERCISE

1 A smoker's blood nicotine level, measure in ng/ml, may be modelled by a normal random variable with mean 310 and standard deviation 110.

(a) What proportion of smokers have blood nicotine levels lower than 250?

(b) What blood nicotine level is exceeded by 20% of smokers? [A]

2 The lengths of components from a machine may be modelled by a normal distribution with mean 65 mm and standard deviation 2 mm. Find the probability that the length of a component selected at random will be less than 67 mm. [A]

3 A health food cooperative markets free-range eggs. Eggs weighing less than 48 g are graded small, those weighing more than 59 g are graded large and the rest are graded medium.

The weight of an egg from a particular supplier is normally distributed with mean 52 g and standard deviation 4 g.

Find:

(a) the proportion of eggs graded small,

(b) the proportion of eggs graded medium,

(c) the median weight of the eggs graded large. [A]

4 Shamim drives from her home in Sale to college in Manchester every weekday during term. On the way she collects her friend David who waits for her at the end of his road in Chorlton. Shamim leaves home at 8.00 a.m., and the time it takes her to reach the end of David's road is normally distributed with mean 23 minutes and standard deviation 5 minutes.

   (a) Find the probability that she arrives at the end of David's road before 8.30 a.m.

   (b) If David arrives at the end of his road at 8.05 a.m. what is the probability that he will have to wait less than 15 minutes for Shamim to arrive?

   (c) What is the latest time, to the nearest minute, that David can arrive at the end of his road to have a probability of at least 0.99 of arriving before Shamim? [A]

5 Free-range eggs supplied by a health food cooperative have a mean weight of 52 g with a standard deviation of 4 g. Assuming the weights are normally distributed find the probability that:

   (a) a randomly selected egg will weigh more than 60 g,

   (b) the mean weight of five randomly selected eggs will be between 50 g and 55 g,

   (c) the mean weight of 90 randomly selected eggs will be between 52.1 g and 52.2 g.

   Which of your answers would be unchanged if the weights are not normally distributed?

6 Bags of sugar are sold as 1 kg. To ensure bags are not sold underweight the machine is set to put a mean weight of 1004 g in each bag. The manufacturer claims that the process works to a standard deviation of 2.4 g. What proportion of bags are underweight?

7 The lengths of components produced by a machine are normally distributed with a mean of 0.984 cm and a standard deviation of 0.006 cm. The specification requires that the length should measure between 0.975 cm and 0.996 cm. Find the probability that a randomly selected component will meet the specification. [A]

8 The weights of bags of fertiliser may be modelled by a normal distribution with mean 12.1 kg and standard deviation 0.4 kg. Find the probability that:

(a) a randomly selected bag will weigh less than 12.0 kg,

(b) the mean weight of four bags selected at random will weigh more than 12.0 kg,

(c) the mean weight of 100 bags will be between 12.0 and 12.1 kg.

How would your answer to **(c)** be affected if the normal distribution was not a good model for the weights of the bags?

9 The weights of plums from an orchard have mean 24 g and standard deviation 5 g. The plums are graded small, medium or large. All plums over 28 g in weight are regarded as large and the rest equally divided between small and medium. Assuming a normal distribution find:

(a) the proportion of plums graded large,

(b) the upper limit of the weights of the plums in the small grade. [A]

10 A survey showed that the value of the change carried by an adult male shopper may be modelled by a normal distribution with mean £3.10 and standard deviation £0.90. Find the probability that:

(a) an adult male shopper selected at random will be carrying between £3 and £4 in change,

(b) the mean amount of change carried by a random sample of nine adult male shoppers will be between £3.00 and £3.05.

Give two reasons why, although the normal distribution may provide an adequate model, it cannot in these circumstances provide an exact model.

11 The weights of pieces of home-made fudge are normally distributed with mean 34 g and standard deviation 5 g.

(a) What is the probability that a piece selected at random weighs more than 40 g?

(b) For some purposes it is necessary to grade the pieces as small, medium or large. It is decided to grade all pieces weighing over 40 g as large and to grade the heavier half of the remainder as medium. The rest will be graded as small. What is the upper limit of the small grade? [A]

12 Yuk Ping belongs to an athletics club. In javelin throwing competitions her throws are normally distributed with mean 41.0 m and standard deviation 2.0 m.

   (a) What is the probability of her throwing between 40 m and 46 m?

   (b) What distance will be exceeded by 60% of her throws?

   Gwen belongs to the same club. In competitions 85% of her javelin throws exceed 35 m and 70% exceed 37.5 m. Her throws are normally distributed.

   (c) Find the mean and standard deviation of Gwen's throws, each correct to two significant figures.

   (d) The club has to choose one of these two athletes to enter a major competition. In order to qualify for the final round it is necessary to achieve a throw of at least 48 m in the preliminary rounds. Which athlete should be chosen and why?   [A]

13 A machine is used to fill tubes, of nominal content 100 ml, with toothpaste. The amount of toothpaste delivered by the machine is normally distributed and may be set to any required mean value. Immediately after the machine has been overhauled, the standard deviation of the amount delivered is 2 ml. As time passes, this standard deviation increases until the machine is again overhauled.

   The following three conditions are necessary for a batch of tubes of toothpaste to comply with current legislation:

   (I) The average content of the tubes must be at least 100 ml.

   (II) Not more than 2.5% of the tubes may contain less than 95.5 ml.

   (III) Not more than 0.1% of the tubes may contain less than 91 ml.

   (a) For a batch of tubes with mean content 98.8 ml and standard deviation 2 ml, find the proportion of tubes which contain:

      (i) less than 95.5 ml,

      (ii) less than 91 ml.

      Hence state which, if any, of the three conditions above are **not** satisfied.

(b) If the standard deviation is 5 ml, find the mean in **each** of the following cases:

   (i) exactly 2.5% of tubes contain less than 95.5 ml,

   (ii) exactly 0.1% of tubes contain less than 91 ml.

   Hence state the smallest value of the mean which would enable all three conditions to be met when the standard deviation is 5 ml.

(c) Currently exactly 0.1% of tubes contain less than 91 ml and exactly 2.5% contain less than 95.5 ml.

   (i) Find the current values of the mean and the standard deviation.

   (ii) State, giving a reason, whether you would recommend that the machine is overhauled immediately. [A]

3

Key point summary

1 The normal distribution is continuous, symmetrical and bell shaped. *p38*

2 The normal distribution with mean 0 and standard deviation 1 is called the standard normal distribution. Tables of this distribution are in the Appendix. *p38*

3 An observation, x, from a normal distribution with mean μ and standard deviation σ is standardised using the formula *p42*

$$z = \frac{x - \mu}{\sigma}.$$

This must be done before the tables can be used.

4 If a random sample of size n is taken from any distribution with mean μ and standard deviation σ, then: *p52*

   • $\bar{x}$, the sample mean, will be distributed with mean μ and standard deviation $\frac{\sigma}{\sqrt{n}}$,

   • the distribution will be approximately normal provided n is reasonably large.

Test yourself	What to review
1 Why do tables of the standard normal distribution not tabulate negative values of *z*?	*Sections 3.1 and 3.4*
2 For a standard normal distribution find the value of *z* which is exceeded with probability: **(a)** 0.06, **(b)** 0.92.	*Section 3.4*
3 A normal distribution has mean 12 and standard deviation 4. Find the probability that an observation from this distribution: **(a)** exceeds 10, **(b)** is less than 5, **(c)** is between 14 and 16, **(d)** is between 8 and 15.	*Section 3.7*
4 What is the probability that an observation from the distribution in question **3** is exactly equal to 10?	*Section 3.1*
5 Under what circumstances may tables of the normal distribution be useful when dealing with a variable which is not normally distributed?	*Section 3.11*
6 A random sample of size 25 is taken from a normal distribution with mean 20 and standard deviation 10. **(a)** Find the probability that the sample mean exceeds 21? **(b)** What value will the mean exceed with a probability of 0.6?	*Section 3.11*
7 Give a reason why, although the normal distribution may provide a good model for the weights of new-born mice, it cannot provide an exact model.	*Section 3.9*

Test yourself **ANSWERS**

7 It is impossible for the mice to have negative weights. A normal distribution would give an infinitesimal but non-zero probability of a baby mouse having a negative weight.

6 (a) 0.309;   **(b)** 19.5.

5 The mean of a large sample will be normally distributed.

4 0.

3 (a) 0.691;   **(b)** 0.0401;   **(c)** 0.150;   **(d)** 0.615.

2 (a) 1.555;   **(b)** −1.405.

1 These are unnecessary as the distribution is symmetrical about zero.

CHAPTER 4
Correlation

Learning objectives

After studying this chapter you should be able to:

■ investigate the strength of a linear relationship between two variables by using suitable statistical analysis

■ evaluate and interpret the product moment correlation coefficient.

4.1 Interpreting scatter diagrams

Interpreting a scatter diagram is often the easiest way for you to decide whether correlation exists. Correlation means that there is a linear relationship between the two variables. This could mean that the points lie on a straight line, but it is much more likely to mean that they are scattered about a straight line.

The four main types of scatter diagram

Positive correlation

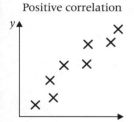

Negative correlation

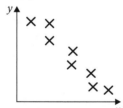

No correlation

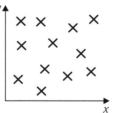

- positive or direct correlation

- negative or inverse correlation

- little or no correlation, no linear relationship

- x increases as y increases

- x decreases as y increases

- x and y are not linked

- clear linear relationship exists.

- clear linear relationship exists.

- x and y appear to be independent.

Non-linear correlation

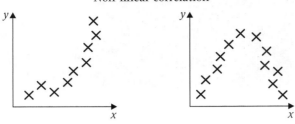

- *x* and *y* are clearly linked by a non-linear relationship.

4.2 Studying results

The table below gives the marks obtained by 10 pupils taking maths and physics tests.

Pupil	A	B	C	D	E	F	G	H	I	J
Maths mark (out of 30) x	20	23	8	29	14	11	11	20	17	17
Physics mark (out of 40) y	30	35	21	33	33	26	22	31	33	36

Is there a connection between the marks obtained by the 10 pupils in the maths and physics tests?

The starting point would be to plot the marks on a scatter diagram.

The areas in the bottom-right and top-left of the graph are almost empty so there is a clear tendency for the points to run from bottom-left to top-right. This indicates that positive correlation exists between *x* and *y*.

Calculating the means:

$$\bar{x} = \frac{170}{10} = 17$$

and

$$\bar{y} = \frac{300}{10} = 30.$$

Using these lines, the graph can be divided into four regions to show this tendency very clearly.

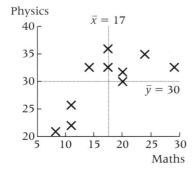

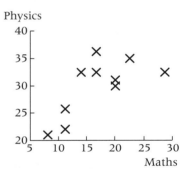

Note the importance of scale.

Consider this change,

The appearance of the scatter diagram is now very different. The existence of correlation is much more difficult to identify. Scales should cover the range of the given data.

The table below gives the marks obtained by the 10 pupils taking maths and history tests.

Pupil	A	B	C	D	E	F	G	H	I	J
Maths mark (out of 30) x	20	23	8	29	14	11	11	20	17	17
History mark (out of 60) z	28	21	42	32	44	56	36	24	51	26

Calculating the mean for z:

$$\bar{z} = \frac{360}{10} = 36$$

The scatter diagram for maths and history shows a clear tendency for points to run from top-left to bottom-right. This indicates that negative correlation exists between x and z.

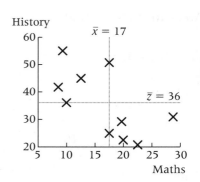

4.3 Product moment correlation coefficient (PMCC)

(This is often known as **Pearson's correlation coefficient** after **Karl Pearson**, an applied mathematician who worked on the application of statistics to genetics and evolution.)

How can the strength of correlation be quantified?

There are two main points to consider:

- how close to a straight line are the points?
- is the correlation positive or negative?

The product moment correlation coefficient, r, gives a standardised measure of correlation which can be used for comparisons between different sets of data.

S_{xx}, S_{yy} and S_{xy} are used to evaluate r where:

$S_{xx} = \sum(x_i - \bar{x})^2$, $S_{yy} = \sum(y_i - \bar{y})^2$ and

$S_{xy} = \sum(x_i - \bar{x})(y_i - \bar{y})$

r is given by $\dfrac{S_{xy}}{\sqrt{S_{xx}S_{yy}}}$

These formulae are given in the AQA formulae book.

Formula

The computational form of this equation which is most commonly used is:

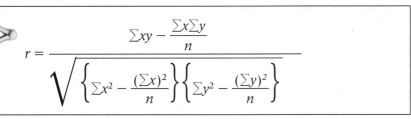

$$r = \frac{\sum xy - \dfrac{\sum x \sum y}{n}}{\sqrt{\left\{\sum x^2 - \dfrac{(\sum x)^2}{n}\right\}\left\{\sum y^2 - \dfrac{(\sum y)^2}{n}\right\}}}$$

r is obtainable directly from all calculators with regression facility. This is permitted in the exam.

Values of *r*

Some worked examples

Returning to the maths and physics marks in section 8.2.

To illustrate the calculation involved in evaluating *r*, the following additional summations are needed:

$$\sum x^2 = 3250, \quad \sum y^2 = 9250, \quad \sum xy = 5313.$$

You can then see that

$$S_{xx} = 3250 - \frac{170^2}{10} = 360$$

and

$$S_{yy} = 9250 - \frac{300^2}{10} = 250$$

Then, $S_{xy} = 5313 - \frac{170 \times 300}{10} = 213$

So

$$r = \frac{213}{\sqrt{360 \times 250}} = 0.71$$

This, of course, can be found directly from your calculator.

The interpretation of the value of *r* is very important. The value of *r* tells you how close the points are to lying on a straight line.

It is always true that:

$$-1 \le r \le +1$$

$r = +1$ indicates **ALL the points lie on a line** with positive gradient

$r = -1$ indicates **ALL the points lie on a line** with negative gradient

$r = 0$ indicates that there is **no linear connection** at all between the two sets of data.

The value obtained in this example, $r = 0.71$, would indicate a fairly strong positive correlation between the test score in maths and the test score in physics.

Sketches to illustrate examples of possible values of *r*.

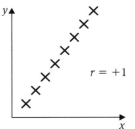
$r = +1$
Exact positive correlation

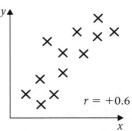
$r = +0.6$
Weak positive correlation

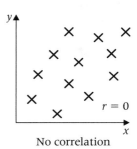
$r = 0$
No correlation

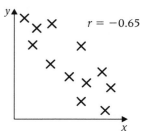
$r = -0.65$
Weak negative correlation

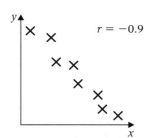
$r = -0.9$
Strong negative correlation

Worked example 4.1

A group of 12 children participated in a psychological study designed to assess the relationship, if any between age, x years, and average total sleep time (ATST), y minutes. To obtain a measure for ATST, recordings were taken on each child on five consecutive nights and then averaged. The results are below.

Child	Age x (years)	ATST y (minutes)
A	4.4	586
B	6.7	565
C	10.5	515
D	9.6	532
E	12.4	478
F	5.5	560
G	11.1	493
H	8.6	533
I	14.0	575
J	10.1	490
K	7.2	530
L	7.9	515

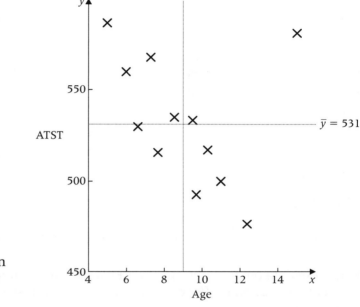

Calculate the product moment correlation coefficient between x and y and interpret your result.

Solution

$\sum x = 108$ and $\sum y = 6372$

$\sum x^2 = 1060.1$, $\sum y^2 = 3\,396\,942$

$\sum xy = 56\,825.4$

$$S_{xx} = 1060.1 - \frac{108^2}{12} = 88.1$$

$$S_{yy} = 3\,396\,942 - \frac{6372^2}{12} = 13\,410$$

Then,

$$S_{xy} = 56\,825.4 - \frac{108 \times 6372}{12} = -522.6$$

So

$$r = \frac{-522.6}{\sqrt{88.1 \times 13\,410}} = -0.481 \text{ (to 3 s.f.)}$$

Considering the value of r and the scatter diagram, there is evidence of weak negative correlation between age and ATST. This would indicate that older children have less ATST than younger children. However, the relationship is fairly weak.

> Note that it would be worth investigating child *I* who seems to have an abnormally high ATST. Perhaps the child was ill during the experiment or perhaps there is some other reason for the excessive amount of sleep.

Worked example 4.2

The following data indicate the level of sales for 10 models of pen sold by a particular company. The sales, together with the selling price of the pen, are given in the table below.

Model	Price, x (£)	Sales, y (00s)
A	2.5	30
B	5	35
C	15	25
D	20	15
E	7.5	25
F	17.5	10
G	12	15
H	6	20
I	25	8
J	30	10

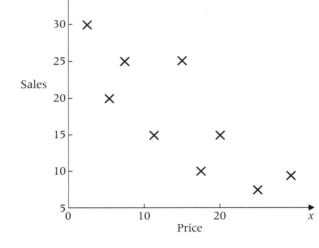

$\sum x = 140.5$ $\sum y = 193$

$\sum x^2 = 2723.75$ $\sum y^2 = 4489$ $\sum xy = 2087.5$

Plot these data on a scatter diagram. Evaluate the product moment correlation coefficient and interpret your answers with reference to the data supplied.

Solution

$$S_{xx} = 2723.75 - \frac{140.5^2}{10} = 749.725$$

$$S_{yy} = 4489 - \frac{193^2}{10} = 764.1$$

Then,

$$S_{xy} = 2087.5 - \frac{140.5 \times 193}{10} = -624.15$$

So

$$r = \frac{-624.15}{\sqrt{749.725 \times 764.1}} = -0.825 \text{ (to 3 s.f.)}$$

Considering the value of r and the scatter diagram, there is evidence of quite strong negative correlation between x and y.

This would indicate that there are fewer sales of the more expensive pens and this trend follows a linear relationship.

Note that care must be taken not to approximate prematurely in calculations or else r may be inaccurate.

Using prematurely rounded figures:

$S_{xx} = 750$ and $S_{yy} = 764$
$S_{xy} = -624$

$$r = \frac{-624}{\sqrt{750 \times 764}}$$

$$= \frac{-624}{757} = -0.824 \text{ (to 3 s.f.)}$$

An error has now occurred. It is only the **final answer** which should be rounded to three significant figures.

4.4 Limitations of correlation

It is very important to remember a few key points about correlation.

Non-linear relationships

> As illustrated in section 4.1, r measures linear relationships only. It is of no use at all when a non-linear relationship is evident. There may well be a very clear relationship between the variables being considered but if that relationship is not linear then r will not help at all.

Note that clear non-linear relationships identified on scatter diagrams should always be commented upon but the evaluation of r is not appropriate.

The scatter diagram should reveal this.

Cause and effect

A student does some research in a primary school and discovers a very strong direct correlation between length of left foot and score in a mental maths test. Does this mean that stretching a child's foot will make them perform better in maths?

Note that any suggestion that correlation may indicate cause and effect in the relationship between two variables should be considered very carefully!

Clearly this is ridiculous and the probable hidden factor is age: older children have bigger feet and a better ability at maths.

> The correlation found between foot length and score in maths is often called *spurious* and should be treated with caution.

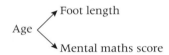

Freak results

> An unusual result can drastically alter the value of r. Unexpected results should always be commented upon and investigated further as their inclusion or exclusion in any calculations can completely change the final result.

Notice the effect on r if the point P is to be removed from correlation calculations using the data below.

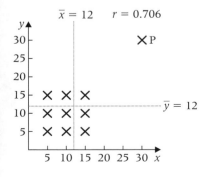

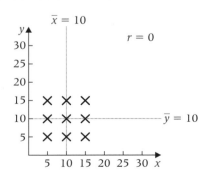

Worked example 4.3

Plot scatter diagrams on separate axes for the following data sets:

(a)

x	15	10	5	20	25	10	25	10
y	3	2.5	5	5	4	5	5	3

(b)

x	2.5	2.8	3	3.2	4.5	5	6	8
y	20	14	10	8	6	4	3	2

It has been suggested that the product moment correlation coefficient should be evaluated for both sets of data. By careful examination of your scatter diagrams, comment on this suggestion in each case.

Solution

(a) The scatter diagram indicates little or no correlation between the two variables. r could be evaluated but would clearly be close to zero.

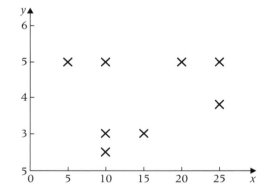

(b) r may well indicate fairly strong negative correlation between the two variables **but** the scatter diagram clearly shows that the relationship is non-linear and hence r is irrelevant.

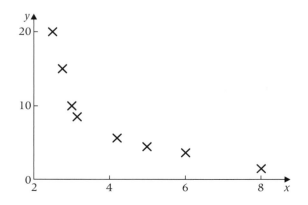

Worked example 4.4 _____

A tasting panel was asked to assess biscuits baked from a new recipe. Each member was asked to assign a score from 0 to 100 for texture (x), for flavour (y) and for sweetness (z).

The scores assigned by the ten tasters were as follows:

Taster	1	2	3	4	5	6	7	8	9	10
x	43	59	76	28	53	55	81	49	38	47
y	67	82	75	48	91	63	67	51	44	54

(a) Draw a scatter diagram to illustrate the data.

(b) Calculate the value of the product moment correlation coefficient between x and y.

(c) State, briefly, how you would expect the scatter diagram to alter if the tasters were given training in how to assign scores before the tasting took place.

(d) Given that $\Sigma z = 601$, $\Sigma z^2 = 38\,637$ and $\Sigma yz = 40\,564$ calculate the product moment correlation coefficient between y and z.

Solution

(a)

> Scatter diagram clearly shows a positive correlation.

(b) $\Sigma x = 529$, $\bar{x} = 52.9$, $\Sigma y = 642$, $\bar{y} = 64.2$

$\Sigma xy = 35\,187$, $\Sigma x^2 = 30\,339$, $\Sigma y^2 = 43\,334$

$$S_{xx} = 30\,339 - \frac{529^2}{10} = 2354.9$$

> Note that a calculator can be used to obtain r directly.

and $S_{yy} = 43\,334 - \dfrac{642^2}{10} = 2117.6$

and $S_{xy} = 35\,187 - \dfrac{529 \times 642}{10} = 1225.2$

therefore, $r = \dfrac{1225.2}{\sqrt{2354.9 \times 2117.6}} = 0.549$ (to 3 s.f.)

(c) The scores would be less variable.

The scatter diagram would be more compact but the overall shape would be similar.

> Training would lead to a more consistent scale for x and y. Without training, people's views on texture or flavour would vary widely.

(d) $\bar{z} = 60.1$, $S_{zz} = 38\,637 - \dfrac{601^2}{10} = 2516.9$

and

$$S_{yz} = 40\,564 - \frac{642 \times 601}{10} = 1979.8$$

> A calculator cannot be used to obtain r directly in this case – the formula must be used.

Therefore,

$$r = \frac{1979.8}{\sqrt{2117.6 \times 2516.9}} = 0.858 \text{ (to 3 s.f.)}$$

> Be careful not to round prematurely.

Worked example 4.5

The following data show the annual income per head, x ($US), and the infant mortality, y (per thousand live births), for a sample of 11 countries.

Country	x	y
A	130	150
B	5950	43
C	560	121
D	2010	53
E	1870	41
F	170	169
G	390	143
H	580	59
I	820	75
J	6620	20
K	3800	39

$\sum x = 22\,900$, $\qquad \sum x^2 = 102\,724\,200$,

$\sum y = 913$, $\qquad \sum y^2 = 103\,517$, $\qquad \sum xy = 987\,130$.

(a) Draw a scatter diagram of the data. Describe the relationship between income per head and infant mortality suggested by the diagram.

(b) An economist asks you to calculate the product moment correlation coefficient.

    (i) Carry out this calculation.

    (ii) Explain briefly to the economist why this calculation may not be appropriate.

Solution

(a)

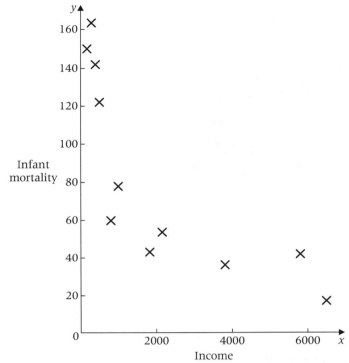

Infant mortality appears to decline as income per head increases.

The decrease is not uniform but is much more marked for the very low incomes than for the higher income countries.

(b) (i) $S_{xx} = 102\,724\,200 - \dfrac{22\,900^2}{11} = 55\,050\,563.64$

and $S_{yy} = 103\,517 - \dfrac{913^2}{11} = 27\,738$

and $S_{xy} = 987\,130 - \dfrac{22\,900 \times 913}{11} = -913\,570$

Therefore, $r = \dfrac{913\,570}{\sqrt{55\,050\,563.64 \times 27\,738}} = -0.739$

(to 3 s.f.)

> Note that this can be found directly from the calculator.

(ii) PMCC measures the strength of a linear relationship. It is not a suitable measure for data which clearly shows a non-linear relationship as in this case.

> A clear curve is seen. See section 4.4.

EXERCISE 4A

1 **(a)** For each of the following scatter diagrams, state whether or not the product moment correlation coefficient is an appropriate measure to use.

(i)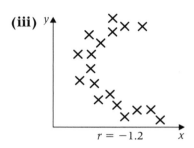

$r = +1$

(ii)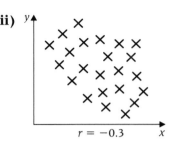

$r = -0.3$

(iii)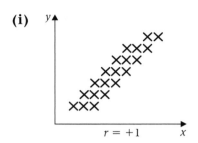

$r = -1.2$

(b) State, giving a reason, whether or not the value underneath each diagram might be a possible value of this correlation coefficient.

2 Estimate, **without undertaking any calculations**, the product moment correlation coefficient between the variables in each of the scatter diagrams given:

(a)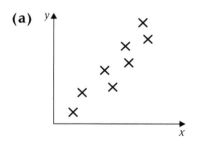

(b)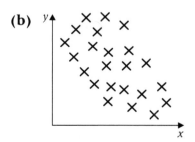

(c)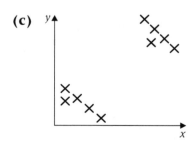

(d)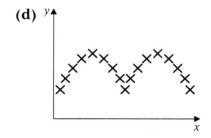

3 For each of the following sets of data:

(a) draw a scatter diagram,

(b) calculate the product moment correlation coefficient between x and y.

(i)

x	1	3	6	10	12
y	5	13	25	41	49

(ii)

x	1	3	6	10	12
y	44	34	24	14	4

(iii)

x	1	1	3	5	5
y	5	1	3	1	5

(iv)

x	1	3	6	9	11
y	12	28	37	28	12

4 The diameters of the largest lichens growing on gravestones were measured.

Age of gravestone (x years)	Diameter of lichen (y mm)
9	2
18	3
20	4
31	20
44	22
52	41
53	35
61	22
63	28
63	32
64	35
64	41
114	51
141	52

(a) Plot a scatter diagram to show the data.

(b) Calculate the values of $\bar{x}$ and $\bar{y}$ and show these as vertical and horizontal lines.

(c) Find the values of S_{xx}, S_{yy} and r.

5 In a biology experiment, a number of cultures were grown in the laboratory. The numbers of bacteria, in millions, and their ages, in days, are given below.

Age (x days)	No. of bacteria (y millions)
1	34
2	106
3	135
4	181
5	192
6	231
7	268
8	300

(a) Plot these data on a scatter diagram with the x-axis having a scale up to 15 days and the y-axis up to 410 million.

(b) Find the value of r, the product moment correlation coefficient.

(c) Some late readings were taken and are given below.

X	13	14	15
Y	400	403	405

Add these points to your scatter diagram and describe what they show.

6 A metal rod was gradually heated and its length, L, was measured at various temperatures, T.

Temperature, T (°C)	Length, L (cm)
15	100
20	103.8
25	106.1
30	112
35	116.1
40	119.9

Draw a scatter diagram to show the data, plotting L against T.

Find the value of r, the product moment correlation coefficient.

It is suspected that a major inaccuracy may have occurred in one or more of the recorded values. Discard any readings which you consider may be untrustworthy and find the new value for r.

Comment on your results.

7 In a workshop producing hand-made goods a score is assigned to each finished item on the basis of its quality (the better the quality the higher the score). The number of items produced by each of 15 craftsmen on a particular day and their average quality score are given below.

Craftsman	No. of items produced, x	Average quality score, y
1	14	6.2
2	23	7.3
3	17	4.9
4	32	7.1
5	16	5.2
6	19	5.7
7	17	5.9
8	25	6.4
9	27	7.3
10	31	6.1
11	17	5.4
12	18	5.7
13	26	6.9
14	24	7.2
15	22	4.8

(a) Draw a scatter diagram to show the data.

(b) Calculate the product moment correlation coefficient between x and y.

(c) The owner of the firm believes that the quality of the output is suffering because some of the craftsmen are working too fast in order to increase bonus payments. Explain to him the meaning of your results, and state what evidence, if any, they provide for or against his belief.

8 During the summer of 1982 the National Leisure Council, on behalf of the Government, conducted a survey into all aspects of the nation's leisure time. The table shows the amount spent per month on sporting pastimes and the total amount spent per month on all leisure activities for a random sample of 13 young married men.

Man	Amount on sport, x	Total amount, y
A	9.0	50.1
B	4.2	46.6
C	12.9	52.4
D	6.1	45.1
E	14.0	56.3
F	1.5	46.6
G	17.4	52.0
H	10.2	48.7
I	18.1	56.0
J	2.9	48.0
K	11.6	54.1
L	15.2	53.3
M	7.3	51.7

(a) Draw a scatter diagram for this data.

(b) Calculate the product moment correlation coefficient for the data.

(c) Comment, with reasons, upon the usefulness, or otherwise, of the above correlation analysis.

9 A clothing manufacturer collected the following data on the age, x months, and the maintenance cost, y (£), of his sewing machines.

Machine	Age, x	Cost, y
A	13	24
B	75	144
C	64	110
D	52	63
E	90	240
F	15	20
G	35	40
H	82	180
I	25	42
J	46	50
K	50	92

(a) Plot a scatter diagram of the data.

(b) Calculate the product moment correlation coefficient.

(c) Comment on your result in **(b)** by making reference to the scatter diagram drawn in **(a)**.

10 The following data relate to a random sample of 15 males, all aged between 40 and 60 years. The measurements given are the level of heart function (out of 100), the percentage of baldness and the average number of hours spent watching television each day.

Male	Heart function	Baldness (%)	Hours of TV
1	42	83	6.2
2	65	66	2.2
3	86	32	1.8
4	32	74	8.3
5	56	69	7.6
6	48	74	6.5
7	92	25	0.8
8	78	30	5.9
9	68	32	2.2
10	52	54	4.4
11	53	58	4.6
12	69	76	2.7
13	57	63	5.8
14	89	38	0.2
15	65	41	4.6

(a) Calculate the value of the product moment correlation coefficient between heart function and percentage baldness.

(b) Calculate the value of the product moment correlation coefficient between heart function and average number of hours of television watched per day.

(c) Comment on the values of the correlation coefficients found in **(a)** and **(b)** and interpret your results.

(d) Do you consider that males aged between 40 and 60 should be advised to reduce the number of hours that they spend watching television in order to ensure a better heart function? Explain your answer.

4

Key point summary

1 A scatter diagram should be drawn to judge whether correlation is present.   *p61*

2 The product moment correlation coefficient,   *p63*

$$r = \frac{\sum xy - \frac{\sum x \sum y}{n}}{\sqrt{\left\{\sum x^2 - \frac{(\sum x)^2}{n}\right\}\left\{\sum y^2 - \frac{(\sum y)^2}{n}\right\}}} \quad \text{or} \quad \frac{S_{xy}}{\sqrt{S_{xx}S_{yy}}}$$

Remember, this can be found directly from a calculator.

r is a measure of **linear** relationship only and $-1 \le r \le +1$

Do not refer to r if a scatter diagram clearly shows a non-linear relationship.

3 $r = +1$ or $r = -1$ implies that the points all **exactly** lie on a **straight line**.   *p64*

$r = 0$ implies **no** linear relationship is present.

But ... no linear relationship between the variables does not necessarily mean that $r = 0$.

4 Even if r is close to $+1$ or -1, **no causal link** should be assumed between the variables without thinking very carefully about the nature of the data involved.   *p67*

Remember the feet stretching! Will it really help you to get better at maths?

Test yourself	**What to review**

1 Which of the following could not be a value for a product moment correlation coefficient?

Section 4.3

(a) $r = 0.98$,

(b) $r = -0.666$,

(c) $r = 1.2$,

(d) $r = 0.003$.

---

2 Which of the following scatter diagrams has a corresponding product moment correlation coefficient given which is not appropriate?

Section 4.3

(a) $r = -0.86$

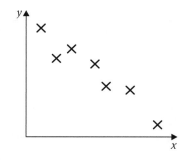

(b) $r = 0.784$

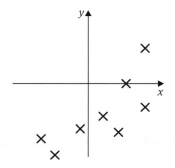

(c) $r = -0.145$

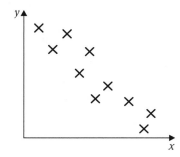

4

Test yourself (*continued*)	What to review

3 For the following data, plot a scatter diagram and evaluate the product moment correlation coefficient.

Section 4.3

x	8	6	5	2	−1	−3	−6
y	−9	−8	−8	0	−5	2	7

4 Explain the meaning of spurious correlation with reference to the following statement:

Section 4.3

'Between 1988 and 1998, the product moment correlation coefficient between the number of incidents of violent juvenile offences taken to court each year and the average number of hours per week which 16- to 19-year-olds spent watching television was found to be 0.874, indicating a high level of correlation.'

5 The weight losses for 10 females enrolled on the same Watch and Weight course at a local Sports Centre are given below.

Section 4.3

Weeks on course	Weight loss (kg)
5	7.6
15	23
12	19.6
3	1.2
10	17.4
8	15.2
20	25.5
10	14
5	2.4
8	9.5

Plot a scatter diagram.

Evaluate the product moment correlation coefficient and comment on its value, referring also to the scatter diagram.

Test yourself ANSWERS

1 (c).

2 (c).

3 $r = -0.904$.

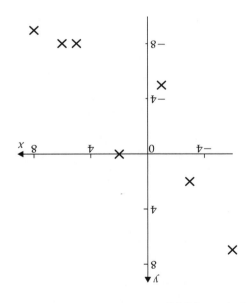

4 Spurious refers to the fact that the link between the two variables may not be causal. They may be two effects from a different cause.

5

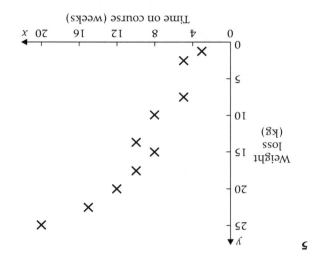

$r = 0.936$. Strong positive correlation. Some suggestion from scatter diagram that weight loss is reaching a peak.

4

CHAPTER 5

Regression

Learning objectives

After studying this chapter you should be able to:
■ find the equation of regression lines using the method of least squares
■ interpret the values obtained for the gradient and intercept of your regression line
■ plot a regression line on a scatter diagram and use the line for prediction purposes
■ calculate residuals and, when appropriate, use them to check the fit of a regression line and to improve predictions.

5

5.1 What is regression analysis?

In linear regression analysis, bivariate data are first examined by drawing a scatter diagram in order to determine whether a linear relationship exists (by eye or by finding the product moment correlation coefficient or PMCC). Then the actual equation of the line of best fit is obtained in the form:

> $y = a + bx$
> This is called the
> **line of y on x**.

This equation may then be used to predict a value of y from a given value of x.

> The regression line is often called the **line of best fit**.

> Remember that we are still considering linear relationships (**straight lines**) only.

> Look back to section 4.1.

> On the scatter diagram, y is plotted on the vertical axis and x on the horizontal.

5.2 Nature of given data

It is always advisable to think about the type of data involved before any regression analysis is started.

For example:

	x	y
1	Height of mother	Height of daughter at age 21
2	Load carried by lorry	Fuel consumption of lorry
3	Breadth of skull	Length of skull

> In pure maths, you may be more familiar with the line equation as
> $y = mx + c$

> In cases **1** and **2**, x can affect y but y can't affect x. Regression line of y on x is appropriate.

> In case **3**, both x and y are influenced by other factors which are not given – correlation is the best analysis.

If y can, sensibly, be predicted from x, then y is called the **dependent** or **response** variable and x is called the **independent** or **explanatory** variable.

Consider cases **1** and **2**.

The scatter diagrams involved might look like these.

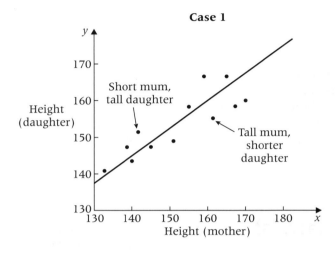

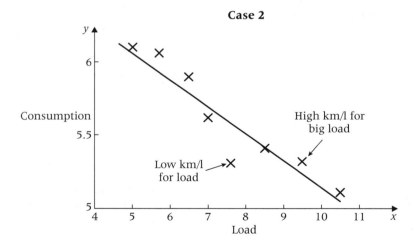

In each case, x is the **explanatory** variable and its values are fixed at the start of the experiment.

Clearly, a mother's height is known well before her daughter reaches the age of 21.

The load to be carried by a lorry would be measured before the trial to find fuel consumption.

Some questions to consider

- How can the regression line be obtained?
- How good is the fit of the line?
- What do the positions of the individual points mean?

The PMCC can be found. See comments on the scatter diagrams.

5.3 Residuals

If you return to case **2**, the data supplied was as follows:

x lorry load (000s kg)	5	5.7	6.5	7	7.6	8.5	9.5	10.5
y fuel consumption (km l^{-1})	6.21	6.12	5.90	5.62	5.25	5.41	5.32	5.11

Note that the fuel consumption is given here in km l^{-1}. A low value indicates that the lorry is using a lot of fuel, while a high value indicates economical fuel usage.

The product moment correlation coefficient (PMCC)

$r = -0.921$ which indicates a strong negative correlation between fuel consumption and load. The points are all close to a straight line.

How close are they and where should the line be placed?

The vertical distances drawn on the scatter diagram are labelled d_i. These are called the **residuals**.

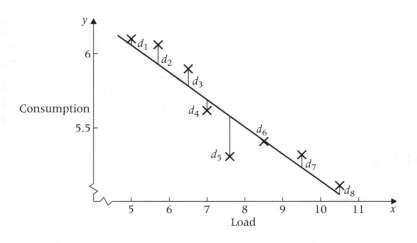

Residuals can be positive (points **above** line) like d_2, d_3, d_7 or negative (points **below** line) like d_4, d_5.

Occasionally, a point might lie exactly on the line.

The residuals measure how far away, for the y values, each point is from the line of best fit. The sum of the squares of these distances is minimised to find the line of regression of y on x.

For each point, the residual is the difference between the observed value of y and the value of y predicted by the line.

5.4 Finding the regression line

The regression line is obtained using the method of least squares and the line is often called the **least squares regression line**.

$d_1^2 + d_2^2 + d_3^2 + \ldots + d_8^2$ or $\sum d_i^2$ is minimised.

The formula is:

$$(y - \bar{y}) = \frac{S_{xy}}{S_{xx}} (x - \bar{x})$$

From this, you should see that the point $(\bar{x}, \bar{y})$ **always** lies on the regression line.

Written in full:

$$(y - \bar{y}) = \frac{\dfrac{\sum xy}{n} - \bar{x}\bar{y}}{\dfrac{\sum x^2}{n} - \bar{x}^2} (x - \bar{x})$$

The regression equation can be obtained directly from a calculator. This is quite acceptable in an exam.

Using the formulae

For these data (section 5.3)

$\bar{x} = 7.5375, \qquad \bar{y} = 5.6175, \qquad n = 8,$

$\sum xy = 333.704, \quad \sum x^2 = 479.25.$

So the equation of regression of y on x using the method of least squares is:

$$(y - 5.6175) = \frac{(\dfrac{1}{8} \times 333.704 - 7.5375 \times 5.6175)}{(\dfrac{1}{8} \times 479.25 - 7.5375^2)} \times (x - 7.5375)$$

Remember that this is an equation connecting x and y. y will remain on the left-hand side and x on the right.

Be very careful not to round prematurely.

So $y - 5.6175 = -0.203\,38\,(x - 7.5375)$

and $y = \mathbf{7.15 - 0.203}x$ is the regression equation.

intercept on y-axis at $x = 0$ ⟵ ⟶ gradient of line

The equation can be obtained directly from a calculator. Check carefully as some calculators give the equation as $y = ax + b$ rather than $y = a + bx$.

5.5 Interpretation of line

The regression line gives some important information about the exact nature of the relationship between x and y.

The gradient and intercept values should always be commented upon by reference to the data involved. In this case:

$a = \mathbf{7.15}$

In this case, comments are required referring to fuel consumption and load.

This intercept value gives an estimate of the amount of fuel consumption, y, when the load, x, is zero. This tells you that the fuel consumption of an unladen lorry is $7.15 \, \text{km l}^{-1}$.

$$b = -0.203$$

7.15 and 0.203 are estimates and are unlikely to be exactly correct.

The gradient indicates, in this case, that y decreases as x increases. Specifically, the fuel consumption, y, decreases by $0.203 \, \text{km l}^{-1}$ for every extra 1000 kg of load.

5.6 Plotting the regression line

As seen earlier, the point $(\bar{x}, \bar{y})$ always lies on the least squares regression line. This point should be plotted on your scatter diagram.

$(\bar{x}, \bar{y}) \approx (7.54, 5.62)$

5

To complete plotting the line accurately, one or preferably two other points should be plotted.

Warning! Never assume that any of the given data points will lie on the line.

Any suitable values for x can be chosen but they need to be spread out over the given range. For example,

$\hat{y}$ means an *estimated* value of y. Many calculators will find $\hat{y}$ directly for a given x.

when $x = 5.5$ gives $\qquad \hat{y} = 6.0 \quad (7.15 - 0.203 \times 5.5)$

and when $x = 10$ gives $\quad \hat{y} = 5.1 \quad (7.15 - 0.203 \times 10)$.

The three points $(5.5, 6.0)$ $(10, 5.1)$ and $(7.54, 5.62)$ can be joined to draw the regression line.

5.7 Further use of residuals

Consider the data we are examining but imagine that more information has now become available. It has been discovered that three different drivers, Ahmed (A), Brian (B) and Carole (C), were involved in the trial. Their individual results were:

Driver	C	B	C	A	A	C	B	B
x load (000s kg)	5	5.7	6.5	7	7.6	8.5	9.5	10.5
y consumption (km l^{-1})	6.21	6.12	5.90	5.62	5.25	5.41	5.32	5.11

The scatter diagram can now be further labelled with this information.

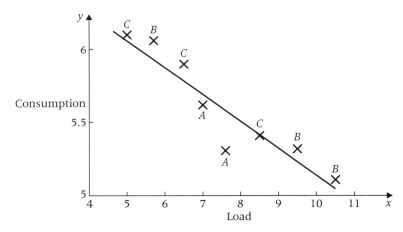

Considering the residual values, further deductions can be made.

It seems that Carole's fuel consumption values lie close to the predicted values given by the line of best fit. However, Ahmed achieves fuel consumption **well below** those predicted by the line and Brian achieves **high** fuel consumption.

This extra information is worth commenting on but always be careful not to make rash judgements, as there may well be other factors involved, for example:

Did all drivers have the same model of lorry?

Did all drivers have the same age of lorry?

Were the journeys of similar length?

Were the journeys over similar types of roads?

It would be very unfair on Ahmed if it was immediately assumed that he was a 'bad' driver and he was sacked.

> **Note:**
> - Use common sense in your interpretations
> - Always refer to the data given.

> You may well think of other factors.

5.8 Predictions

How could the transport manager of the freight company that Ahmed, Brian and Carole work for, use the regression line to predict the fuel consumption for the delivery of a specific load?

Several factors need to be considered:

- How close to the line are the points – is the regression line a 'good fit'?
- Is it sensible to predict y from x?
- What is the range of the x-values given from which the line was calculated?
- What is the size of the x-value from which a value of y is to be predicted?

> PMCC measures this, see chapter 4.

> Look back to section 4.2.

> These are the x-values given in the table of results.

For any regression line where the fit is good, and it is sensible to predict y from x, a value of y can be obtained by substituting a value of x into $y = a + bx$.

There are **limitations** to these predictions however.

Look at this scatter diagram where the scale on the x-axis has been extended.

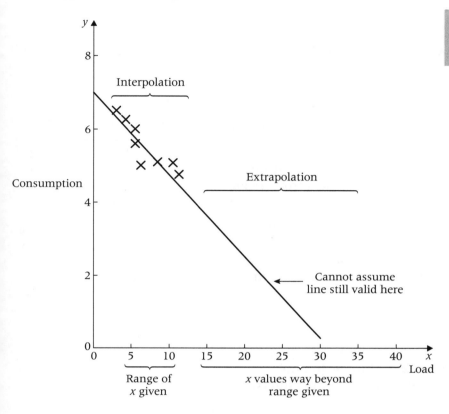

Interpolation

It is perfectly valid to use the least squares regression line $y = 7.15 - 0.203x$ to predict fuel consumption for loads between 5000 and 10 500 kg.

($5 \leq x \leq 10.5$ is the given range).

This is called **interpolation**.

For example, to find the predicted fuel consumption for a load of 8000 kg.

8000 kg means $x = 8$.

$$\hat{y} = 7.15 - 0.203 \times 8 = 5.53 \text{ km l}^{-1} \text{ (to 3 s.f.).}$$

$\hat{y}$ is the notation for an *estimated* value of y, see Section 5.6.

Extrapolation

Could the fuel consumption be predicted if the load was 30 000 kg ($x = 30$)?

Clearly, common sense would indicate that this load is enormous compared to those loads given in the original data. The lorry would probably collapse under the weight!

? Fuel consumption

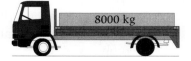

Predicting *y* from *x*, when *x* is outside the range of given data is called **extrapolation** and is very dangerous as the *y*-value obtained is likely to be completely inaccurate.

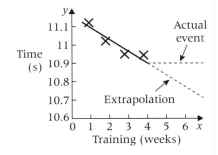

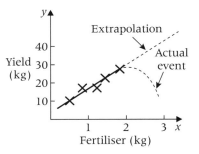

Examples

This scatter diagram shows the time in seconds to run 100 m against the number of weeks of intensive training undertaken by the athlete.

There appears to be a linear relationship but clearly this cannot continue indefinitely. The number of seconds taken to run 100 m will not keep on decreasing but will probably level off when the athlete is fully fit and trained for the event.

The second scatter diagram illustrates a possible relationship between the amount of fertiliser used and the yield from a plot of tomato plants.

Again, it appears that there is a strong linear relationship between yield and amount of fertiliser, but clearly the yield will not continue to increase in this way and, in fact, it will probably decline as too much fertiliser may well lead to a decrease in tomato yield.

Worked example 5.1

1 An electric fire was turned on in a cold room and the temperature of the room was noted at five-minute intervals.

Time from switching on fire, *x* (min)	0	5	10	15	20	25	30	35	40
Temperature, *y* (°C)	0.4	1.5	3.4	5.5	7.7	9.7	11.7	13.5	15.4

(a) Plot the data on a scatter diagram.

(b) Calculate the line of regression $y = a + bx$ and draw it on your scatter diagram.

(c) Predict the temperature 60 minutes from switching on the fire. Why should this prediction be treated with caution?

(d) Explain why, in **(b)** the line $y = a + bx$ was calculated.

(e) If, instead of the temperature being measured at five-minute intervals, the time for the room to reach predetermined temperatures (e.g. 1, 4, 7, 10, 13°C) had been observed, what would the appropriate calculation have been?

Solution

(a)

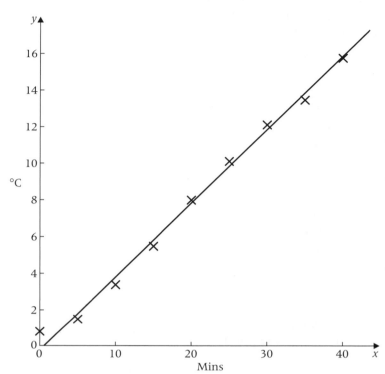

(b) $y = -0.142 + 0.389x$

$\bar{x} = 20, \bar{y} = 7.64,$ plot $(20, 7.64)$

$x = 10, \hat{y} = 3.75,$ plot $(10, 3.75)$

$x = 37.5, \hat{y} = 14.46,$ plot $(37.5, 14.46)$

(c) $x = 60, \hat{y} = 23.2.$

Treat with caution because 60 minutes is outside the range of times given. The linear model cannot continue indefinitely as the room cannot keep on heating up forever.

(d) The line $y = a + bx$, the equation of temperature on time, was used because y depended on the value of x. The dependent variable y was observed at predetermined values of the explanatory variable x.

(e) If the time to reach a temperature was observed, then x would be observed at predetermined values for y. In this case, x would depend on the value of y, so an equation of time on temperature would be appropriate.

> The equation of the line of regression can be obtained directly from a calculator.

> $\hat{y}$ can be obtained from a calculator or by substituting into the regression equation, so for $x = 10$,
> $$\hat{y} = -0.142 + 3.89 \times 10 = 3.75$$

5

Worked example 5.2

The following data refer to a particular developed country. The table shows for each year, the annual average temperature $x°C$, and an estimate of the total annual domestic energy consumption, y PJ (peta-joules).

Year	x	y
1984	9.6	1664
1985	9.3	1715
1986	9.8	1622
1987	10.3	1624
1988	10.1	1621
1989	10.4	1588
1990	10.8	1577
1991	9.7	1719
1992	10.7	1604
1993	9.2	1811
1994	9.8	1754

(a) Illustrate the relationship between energy consumption and temperature by a scatter diagram. Label the points according to the year.

(b) Calculate the line of regression of y on x and draw the line on your scatter diagram.

(c) Use your equation to estimate the energy consumption in 1995, given that the average temperature in that year was 10.3°C.

(d) Calculate residuals for each of the years 1991, 1992, 1993 and 1994. Comment on their values and interpret the pattern shown by the scatter diagram.

(e) Modify your estimate of energy consumption in 1995 in the light of the residuals you have calculated.

Solution

(a)

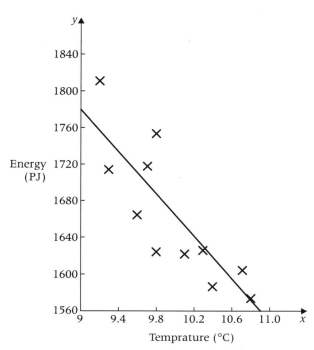

(b) $y = 2849 - 118.9x$

$\bar{x} = 9.97, \bar{y} = 1663.5$, plot $(9.97, 1663.5)$

$x = 9, \hat{y} = 1778.9$, plot $(9, 1778.9)$

$x = 10, \hat{y} = 1660$, plot $(10, 1660)$

(c) Prediction for 1995

$x = 10.3 \quad \hat{y} = 1625$

(d) Residuals are obtained in the following way.

Year	y	x	$\hat{y} =$ $2849 - 118.9x$	Residual = $y - \hat{y}$
1991	1719	9.7	1695.7	23.3
1992	1604	10.7	1576.8	27.2
1993	1811	9.2	1755.1	55.9
1994	1754	9.8	1683.8	70.2

The residuals seem to be increasing with time. The scatter diagram suggests that fuel consumption decreases as the average temperature increases. There is also an increase in fuel consumption with time.

(e) The modified estimate for 1995 would be

$$1625 + 85 = 1710.$$

The regression equation can be obtained directly from a calculator.

Obtain $\hat{y}$ from a calculator or by substituting into the equation as in the previous example.

Residuals can be found using the equation or by reading off the vertical difference between the value of y given by the line and the observed value of y.

Clear, common sense comments are needed.

The residuals found in **(d)** clearly indicate a higher value would be expected in 1995.
A sensible suggestion would be to add a residual value on to the 1625 prediction. This value will be greater than 70.2 for 1994. Continuing the pattern, approx. $70.2 + 15 = 85$ might be the residual in 1995.

EXERCISE 5A

1 The heart and body mass of 14 10-month-old male mice are given in the following table.

Body mass (x) g	Heart mass (y) mg
27	118
30	136
37	156
38	150
32	140
36	155
32	157
32	114
38	144
42	159
36	149
44	170
33	131
38	160

(a) Draw a scatter diagram of these data.

(b) Calculate the line of regression of heart mass on body mass (y on x).

2 The systolic blood pressure of 10 men of various ages are given in the following table.

Age, x (years)	Systolic blood pressure, y (mm Hg)
37	110
35	117
41	125
43	130
42	138
50	146
49	148
54	150
60	154
65	160

(a) Draw a scatter diagram.

(b) Find the line of regression of systolic blood pressure on age.

(c) Use your line to predict the systolic blood pressure for a man who is:
   (i) 20 years old,
   (ii) 45 years old.

(d) Comment on the likely accuracy of your predictions in (i) and (ii).

3 A scientist, working in an agricultural research station, believes that there is a relationship between the hardness of the shells of the eggs laid by chickens and the amount of a certain food supplement put into the diet of the chickens. He selects ten chickens of the same breed and collects the following data.

Chicken	Amount of supplement, x g	Hardness of shell, y
A	7.0	1.2
B	9.8	2.1
C	11.6	3.4
D	17.5	6.1
E	7.6	1.3
F	8.2	1.7
G	12.4	3.4
H	17.5	6.2
I	9.5	2.1
J	19.5	7.1

(Hardness is measured on a scale of 0–10, 10 being the hardest. No units are attached.)

(a) Draw a scatter diagram to illustrate these data.

(b) Calculate the equation of the regression line of hardness on amount of supplement.

(c) Do you believe that this linear model will continue to be appropriate no matter how large or small x becomes? Justify your reply.

4 In an investigation into predictions using the stars, a well-known astrologer, Horace Scope, predicted the ages at which 13 young people would first marry. The completed data, of predicted and actual ages at first marriage, are now available and are summarised in the following table.

Person	Predicted age, x years	Actual age, y years
A	24	23
B	30	31
C	28	28
D	36	35
E	20	20
F	22	25
G	31	45
H	28	30
I	21	22
J	29	27
K	40	40
L	25	27
M	27	26

(a) Draw a scatter diagram of these data.

(b) Calculate the line of regression of y on x.

(c) Plot the regression line on the scatter diagram.

(d) Comment on the results obtained, particularly in view of the data for person G. What further action would you suggest?

5 The given data relate to the price and engine capacity of new cars in January 1982.

Car model	Price (£) y	Capacity (cc) x
A	3900	1000
B	4200	1270
C	5160	1750
D	6980	2230
E	6930	1990
F	2190	600
G	2190	650
H	4160	1500
J	3050	1450
K	6150	1650

(a) Plot a scatter diagram of the data.

(b) Calculate the line of regression of y on x.

(c) Draw the line of regression on the scatter diagram.

(d) A particular customer regards large engine capacity and a low price as the two most important factors in choosing a car. Examine your scatter diagram and the regression line to suggest to him one model which, in January 1982, gave good value for money. Also suggest three models which you would advise the customer not to buy.

6 A small firm tries a new approach to negotiating the annual pay rise with each of its 12 employees. In an attempt to simplify the process, it is suggested that each employee should be assigned a score, x, based on his/her level of responsibility. The annual salary will be £($bx + a$) and negotiations will only involve the values of a and b.

The following table gives last year's salaries (which were generally regarded as fair) and the proposed scores.

Employee	x	Annual salary (£) y
A	10	5750
B	55	17 300
C	46	14 750
D	27	8200
E	17	6350
F	12	6150
G	85	18 800
H	64	14 850
I	36	9900
J	40	11 000
K	30	9150
L	37	10 400

(a) Plot the data on a scatter diagram.

(b) Estimate the values that could have been used for a and b last year by finding the line of regression of y on x.

(c) Comment on whether the suggested method is likely to prove reasonably satisfactory in practice.

(d) Two employees, B and C, had to work away from home for a large part of the year. In the light of this additional information, suggest an improvement to the model.

7 A company specialises in supplying 'stocking fillers' at Christmas time. The company employs several full-time workers all year round but it relies on part-time help at the Christmas rush period.

The time taken to pack orders, together with the packer concerned and the number of items in the order were recorded for orders chosen at random during three days just prior to Christmas.

Packer	No. of items x	Time to pack y (mins)
Ada	21	270
Ada	62	420
Betty	30	245
Alice	20	305
Ada	35	320
Ada	57	440
Alice	40	400
Betty	10	180
Ada	48	350
Alice	58	490
Ada	20	285
Betty	45	340

(a) Plot a scatter diagram to illustrate these data. Label clearly which packer was responsible for the order.

(b) Calculate the value of the product moment correlation coefficient and comment on its value.

(c) Find the line of regression of y on x.

(d) Find an estimate for the length of time that it would take to pack an order of 45 items. Comment on how good an estimate you would imagine this to be.

(e) Calculate the residual values for Betty and also for her daughter Alice, who is working in the factory on a temporary basis over the Christmas holiday.

Use these residuals to produce a better estimate of the actual time expected for the next order of 45 items to be assembled if:

(i) Betty is the packer,

(ii) Alice is the packer.

8 Over a period of three years, a company has been monitoring the number of units of output produced per quarter and the total cost of producing the units. The table below shows the results.

Units of output, x (1000s)	Total cost, y (£1000)
14	35
29	50
55	73
74	93
11	31
23	42
47	65
69	86
18	38
36	54
61	81
79	96

(a) Draw a scatter diagram of these data.

(b) Calculate the equation of the regression line of y on x and draw this line on your scatter diagram.

The selling price of each unit of output is £1.60.

(c) Use your graph to estimate the level of output at which the total income and the total costs are equal.

(d) Give a brief interpretation of this value.

9 In the development of a new plastic material, a variable of interest was its 'deflection' when subjected to a constant force underwater. It was believed that, over a limited range of temperatures, this would be approximately linearly related to the temperature of the water. The 'deflection' was measured at a series of predetermined temperatures with the following results.

Technician	'Deflection' y	Temperature $x\,(^\circ\text{C})$
A	2.05	15
B	2.45	20
A	2.50	25
C	2.00	30
B	3.25	35
A	3.20	40
C	4.50	45
B	3.85	50
A	3.70	55
C	3.65	60

5

(a) Illustrate this data with a scatter diagram.

(b) Calculate the equation of the regression line of 'deflection' on temperature and draw this line on your scatter diagram.

(c) Three different technicians, A, B and C, were involved in the trial. Label your scatter diagram with this information and comment on the performance of each technician.

(d) Suggest what action might be taken before conducting further trials.

10 In addition to its full-time staff, a supermarket employs part-time sales staff on Saturdays. The manager experimented to see if there is a relationship between the takings and the number of part-time staff employed.

He collected data over nine successive Saturdays.

Number of part-time staff employed, x	Takings, £'00 y
10	313
13	320
16	319
19	326
22	333
25	342
28	321
31	361
34	355

(a) Plot a scatter diagram of these data.

(b) Calculate the equation of the regression line of takings on the number of part-time staff employed. Draw the line on your scatter diagram.

(c) If the regression line is denoted by $y = a + bx$, give an interpretation to each of a and b.

(d) On one Saturday, major roadworks blocked a nearby road. Which Saturday do you think this was? Give a reason for your choice.

(e) The manager had increased the number of part-time staff each week. This was desirable from an organisational point of view but undesirable from a statistical point of view. Comment.

Key point summary

1 A scatter diagram should be drawn to judge whether *p83* linear regression analysis is a sensible option.

2 The nature of the data should be considered to *p84* determine which is the *independent* or *explanatory* variable (*x*) and which is the *dependent* or *response* variable (*y*).

3 The regression line is found using the *method of* *p86* *least squares* in the form

$$y = \mathbf{a} + \mathbf{b}x$$

This is the regression line of *y* on *x* and may be used to predict a value for *y* from a given value of *x*.

The equations can be found directly from a calculator with a linear regression mode.

Be careful to note the form in which your calculator presents the equation – it may be as $y = \mathbf{a}x + \mathbf{b}$.

4 **a** estimates the value of *y* when *x* is zero. *pp86, 87*
b estimates the rate of change of *y* with *x*.

5 Be very careful when predicting from your line. *p90* Watch out for extrapolation when predictions can be wildly inaccurate.

Look back to section 5.8.

Never assume a linear model will keep on going forever.

Test yourself   ## What to review

1 For each of the following sets of data say which variable is the *Section 5.2* response or dependent variable, and which is the explanatory or independent variable.

(a)

Temperature required, *w* (°C)	Time taken to reach required temp, *u* (min)
15	4.3
20	8.7
25	11.9
30	14.8
35	17.1

Test yourself (continued)	**What to review**

(b)

Time fire has been switched on, f (min)	Temperature reached g (°C)
5	12.2
10	14.6
15	16.1
20	17.8
25	19.3

2 Which of the following scatter diagrams could illustrate data connected by the given regression equations?

Section 5.1

(a) $y = -6x + 12.3$

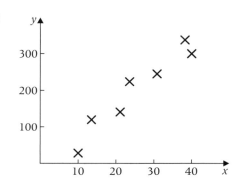

(b) $p = 0.78t - 2.1$

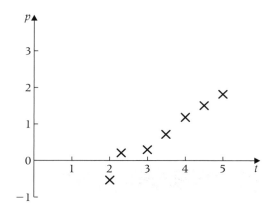

(c) $m = 0.15b - 1.9$

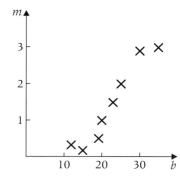

Test yourself (continued)	**What to review**

3 The line of regression of mass (y kg) on age (x weeks) for baby giraffes, between 0 and 12 weeks of age, is given below:

$$y = 2.07x + 21.7$$

Sections 5.2 and 5.5

  (a) Is it possible to obtain an estimate of the mass of a baby giraffe at 9 weeks old from this equation?

  (b) Is it possible to estimate the age in weeks of a baby giraffe which has mass 42 kg?

  (c) Interpret the value of the constant 21.7 in this equation.

4 The table below gives the height of a bean shoot in cm (y) and the number of days since it was planted (x).

Sections 5.4 and 5.8

Number of days, x	Height, y (cm)
40	9.6
45	10.5
50	11.2
55	12.3
60	13.4
65	14.3
70	15.2

  (a) Calculate the line of regression of y on x.

  (b) Estimate the height of the shoot exactly eight weeks (56 days) after planting.

  (c) Why would it not be sensible to use the regression equation to estimate the height of the shoot three months after planting?

5

5 As part of his research into the behaviour of the human memory, a leading psychologist asked 15 schoolgirls from years 9, 10 and 11 to talk for five minutes on 'my day at school'. The psychologist asked each girl to record how many times she thought she had used the word 'nice' during the talk. The following table gives their replies together with the true values.

Section 5.3

Girl	True value x	Recorded value y
A	12	9
B	20	19
C	1	3
D	8	14
E	0	4
F	12	12
G	12	16
H	17	14
I	6	5
J	5	9
K	24	20
L	23	16
M	10	11
N	18	17
O	16	19

The equation of the regression line of y on x is $y = 4.40 + 0.663x$.

The girls are from three different year groups.

A, *C*, *H*, *I* and *L* are from Year 11.

E, *F*, *K*, *M* and *N* are from Year 10.

B, *D*, *G*, *J* and *O* are from Year 9.

Find the residuals for the girls in Year 9 and for those in Year 11. Use these, together with the regression line to estimate:

(a) the recorded value for a girl in Year 9 whose true value was 15,

(b) the recorded value for a girl in Year 11 whose true value was 10.

Test yourself ANSWERS

1 (a) Explanatory: temperature, dependent: time

   (b) Explanatory: time, dependent: temperature.

2 (a) No;   (b) Yes;   (c) Yes;

3 (a) Yes;

   (b) No (line has y as dependent not x);

   (c) Mass at birth: 21.7 kg.

4 (a) $y = 0.190x + 1.91$;

   (b) $y = 0.190 \times 56 + 1.91 = 12.6$ cm;

   (c) At 3 months, extrapolation would be used and therefore results may be very inaccurate as linear model may not continue.

5 Residuals: B 1.3, D 4.3, G 3.6, J 1.3, O 4.0, A -3.4, C -2.1, H -1.7, I -3.4, L -3.7.

(a) 17; (b) 8.

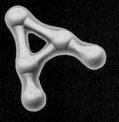

CHAPTER 6

Confidence intervals

Learning objectives

After reading this chapter you should be able to:

- calculate a confidence interval for the mean of a normal distribution with a known standard deviation
- calculate a confidence interval for the mean of any distribution from a large sample.

6.1 Introduction

Applying statistics often involves using a sample to draw conclusions about a population. This is known as statistical inference. There are two main methods of statistical inference: confidence intervals, which are the subject of this chapter, and hypothesis testing, which is the subject of chapter 7. Confidence intervals are used when we wish to estimate a population parameter and hypothesis testing is used when we wish to make a decision. The calculations involved in the two methods are often similar but the purpose is different.

6.2 Confidence interval for the mean of a normal distribution, standard deviation known

The method is best understood by considering a specific example.

The contents of a large batch of packets of baking powder are known to be normally distributed with standard deviation 7 g. The mean is unknown. A randomly selected packet is found to contain 193 g of baking powder. If this is the only information available the best estimate of the mean contents of the batch is 193 g. This is called a point estimate. However we know that if a different packet had been selected it would almost certainly have contained a different amount of baking powder. It is better to estimate the mean by an interval rather than by a single value. The interval expresses the fact that there is only a limited amount of information and so there is uncertainty in the estimate.

If an observation is taken from a standard normal distribution there is a probability of 0.95 that it will lie in the range ±1.96.

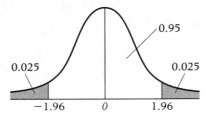

This means that there is a probability of 0.95 that an observation, x, from a normal distribution with mean μ and standard deviation σ will lie in the interval $\mu \pm 1.96\sigma$.

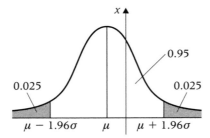

In the example of the packets of baking powder the value of x is known but the value of μ is unknown. If the interval is centred on x, i.e. $x \pm 1.96\sigma$, there is a probability of 0.95 that this interval will contain μ.

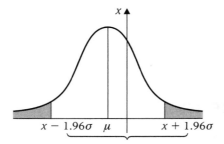

For the packets of baking powder the interval is

$$193 \pm 1.96 \times 7$$

i.e. 193 ± 13.7 or 179.3 to 206.7.

The interval is called a 95% confidence interval. This is because if intervals are calculated in this way then, in the long run, 95% of the intervals calculated will contain the population mean. This also means that 5% will not contain the population mean. Unfortunately there is no way of knowing, in a particular case, whether the interval calculated is one of the 95% which does contain μ or one of the 5% which does not contain μ. You can however say that it is much more likely to contain μ than not to contain μ.

The population mean, μ, is constant but unknown. The interval is known but will be different for each observation, x.

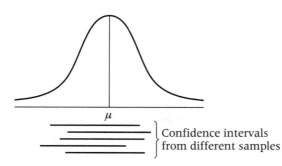

Confidence intervals from different samples

The level of confidence can be increased by widening the interval. For example a 99% confidence interval is

$$193 \pm 2.5758 \times 7$$

i.e. 193 ± 18.0 or 175.0 to 211.0.

It is not possible to calculate a 100% confidence interval.

> This is because there are no limits which contain 100% of a normal distribution.

Intuitively, it seems that a better estimate of μ, the mean contents of the packets of baking powder, will be obtained if we weigh the contents of more than one packet.

Four randomly selected packets were found to contain 193, 197, 212 and 184 g of baking powder. The sample mean is 196.5. The standard deviation of the mean of a sample of size four is $\dfrac{7}{\sqrt{4}} = 3.5$.

A 95% confidence interval for the population mean is

$$196.5 \pm 1.96 \times 3.5$$

i.e. 196.5 ± 6.9 or 189.6 to 203.4.

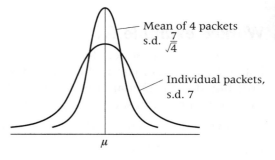

Mean of 4 packets
s.d. $\dfrac{7}{\sqrt{4}}$

Individual packets, s.d. 7

μ

Note 1. This interval is half the width of the 95% confidence interval calculated from the weight of a single packet. This has been achieved by increasing the sample size from one to four. However there is very little advantage in increasing a sample of size 21 to one of size 24. To halve the width of the interval you need to **multiply** the sample size by four.

Note 2. If the distribution is not normal the confidence interval will be inaccurate. This could be a major problem for the single observation but would be less serious for the sample of size four. For large samples the sample mean will be approximately normally distributed. Four is not a large sample but the mean of a sample of size four will come closer to following a normal distribution than will the distribution of a single observation.

> If $\bar{x}$ is the mean of a random sample of size n from a normal distribution with (unknown) mean μ and (known) standard deviation σ, a $100(1 - \alpha)\%$ confidence interval for μ is given by $\bar{x} \pm z_{\frac{\alpha}{2}} \dfrac{\sigma}{\sqrt{n}}$.

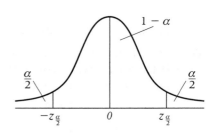

Worked example 6.1

A machine fills bottles with vinegar. The volumes of vinegar contained in these bottles are normally distributed with standard deviation 6 ml.

A random sample of five bottles from a large batch filled by the machine contained the following volumes, in millilitres, of vinegar:

986   996   984   990   1002

Calculate a 90% confidence interval for the mean volume of vinegar in bottles of this batch.

Solution

Sample mean = 991.6 ml
90% confidence interval for mean

$$991.6 \pm 1.6449 \times \frac{6}{\sqrt{5}}$$

i.e. 991.6 ± 4.41 or 987.2 to 996.0 ml

0.9

0.05   0.05

−1.6499   0   1.6499

Answers are usually given to 3 s.f. In this case, because the limits of the interval are close together 4 s.f is reasonable.

Worked example 6.2

A food processor produces large batches of jars of jam. In each batch the weight of jam in a jar is known to be normally distributed with standard deviation 7 g. The weights, in grams, of the jam in a random sample of jars from a particular batch were:

481   455   468   457   469   463   469   458

(a) Calculate a 95% confidence interval for the mean weight of jam in this batch of jars.

(b) Assuming the mean weight is at the upper limit of the confidence interval calculated in **(a)**, calculate the limits within which 99% of weights of jam in these jars lies.

(c) The jars are claimed to contain 454 g of jam. Comment on this claim as it relates to this batch.

Solution

(a) Sample mean = 465.0
95% confidence interval for mean weight of jam is

$$465 \pm 1.96 \times \frac{7}{\sqrt{8}}$$

i.e. 465 ± 4.851 or 460.1 to 469.9

(b) The upper limit of the confidence interval is 469.9.
If the mean were 469.9, 99% of the weights of jam in the jars would lie in the range

$$469.9 \pm 2.5758 \times 7$$

i.e. 469.9 ± 18.0 or 451.9 to 487.9.

Again 4 s.f. is reasonable.

Here we are dealing with individual jars, not with sample means.

(c) 454 is below the lower limit of the confidence interval calculated in **(a)**. Hence it is safe to assume that the **mean** weight of jam in the jars exceeds 454 g.

However even if it is assumed that the mean is at the upper limit of the confidence interval, the interval calculated in **(b)** shows that some individual jars will contain less than 454 g.

EXERCISE 6A

1 The potency of a particular brand of aspirin tablets is known to be normally distributed with standard deviation 0.83. A random sample of tablets of this brand was tested and found to have potencies of

　　58.7　58.4　59.3　60.4　59.8　59.4　57.7　60.3　61.0　58.2

Calculate:

(a) a 99% confidence interval for the mean potency of these tablets,

(b) a 95% confidence interval for the mean potency of these tablets,

(c) a 60% confidence interval for the mean potency of these tablets.

2 The diastolic blood pressures, in millimetres of mercury, of a population of healthy adults has standard deviation 12.8. The diastolic blood pressures of a random sample of members of an athletics club were measured with the following results:

　　79.2　　64.6　　86.8　　73.7　　74.9　　62.3

(a) Assuming the sample comes from a normal distribution with standard deviation 12.8 calculate:

　(i) a 90% confidence interval for the mean,

　(ii) a 95% confidence interval for the mean,

　(iii) a 99% confidence interval for the mean.

The diastolic blood pressures of a random sample of members of a chess club were also measured with the following results:

　　84.6　　93.2　　104.6　　106.7　　76.3　　78.2

(b) Assuming the sample comes from a normal distribution with standard deviation 12.8 calculate:

　(i) an 80% confidence interval for the mean,

　(ii) a 95% confidence interval for the mean,

　(iii) a 99% confidence interval for the mean.

(c) Comment on the diastolic blood pressure of members of each of the two clubs given that a population of healthy adults would have a mean of 84.8.

3 Applicants for an assembly job are to be given a test of manual dexterity. The times, in seconds, taken by a random sample of applicants to complete the test are

63   229   165   77   49   74   67   59   66   102   81   72   59

Calculate a 90% confidence interval for the mean time taken by applicants. Assume the data comes from a normal distribution with standard deviation 57 s.

4 A rail traveller records the time she has to queue to buy a ticket. A random sample of times, in seconds, were

136   120   67   255   84   99   280   55   78

(a) Assuming the data may be regarded as a random sample from a normal distribution with standard deviation 44 s, calculate a 95% confidence interval for the mean queuing time.

(b) Assume that the mean is at the lower limit of the confidence interval calculated in **(a)**. Calculate limits within which 90% of her waiting times will lie.

(c) Comment on the station manager's claim that most passengers have to queue for less than 25 s to buy a ticket.

5 A food processor produces large batches of jars of pickles. In each batch, the gross weight of a jar is known to be normally distributed with standard deviation 7.5 g. (The gross weight is the weight of the jar plus the weight of the pickles.)
The gross weights, in grams, of a random sample from a particular batch were:

514   485   501   486   502   496   509   491   497
501   506   486   498   490   484   494   501   506
490   487   507   496   505   498   499

(a) Calculate a 90% confidence interval for the mean gross weight of this batch.

The weight of an empty jar is known to be exactly 40 g.

(b) (i) What is the standard deviation of the weight of the pickles in a batch of jars?

(ii) Assuming that the mean gross weight is at the upper limit of the confidence interval calculated in **(a)**, calculate limits within which 99% of the weights of the pickles would lie.

(c) The jars are claimed to contain 454 g of pickles. Comment on this claim as it relates to this batch of jars.

6.3 Confidence interval for the mean based on a large sample

There are not many real life situations where we wish to use a confidence interval to estimate an unknown population mean when the population standard deviation is known. In most cases where the mean is unknown the standard deviation will also be unknown. If a large sample is available then this will provide a sufficiently good estimate of the standard deviation to enable a confidence interval for the mean to be calculated. The large sample also has the advantage of the sample mean being approximately normally distributed no matter what the distribution of the individual items.

> This could occur in a mass production process where the mean length of components depends on the machine settings but the standard deviation is always the same. However it is unusual.

If a large random sample is available:

- it can be used to provide a good estimate of the population standard deviation σ,
- it is safe to assume that the mean is normally distributed.

> The definition of 'large' is arbitrary. A rule of thumb is that 'large' means at least 30.

6

Worked example 6.3

Seventy packs of butter, selected at random from a large batch delivered to a supermarket, are weighed. The mean weight is found to be 227 g and the standard deviation is found to be 7.5 g. Calculate a 95% confidence interval for the mean weight of all packs in the batch.

> The sample is large and so it makes little difference whether the divisor n or $n - 1$ is used in calculating the standard deviation. Both will give very similar results. As the population standard deviation is being estimated from a sample it is correct to use the divisor $n - 1$.

Solution

Seventy is a large sample and so although the standard deviation of the weights is not known we may use the standard deviation calculated from the sample. It does not matter whether the distribution is normal or not since the mean of a sample of 70 from any distribution may be modelled by a normal distribution.

The 95% confidence interval for the mean weight of packs of butter in the batch is

$$227 \pm 1.96 \times \frac{7.5}{\sqrt{70}}$$

i.e. 227 ± 1.76 or 225.2 to 228.8.

> At least 4 s.f. are required here. If the answer was rounded to 2 s.f. the interval would disappear completely.

Worked example 6.4

Shoe shop staff routinely measure the length of their customers' feet. Measurements of the length of one foot (without shoes) from each of 180 adult male customers yielded a mean length of 29.2 cm and a standard deviation of 1.47 cm.

(a) Calculate a 95% confidence interval for the mean length of male feet.

(b) Why was it not necessary to assume that the lengths of feet are normally distributed in order to calculate the confidence interval in **(a)**?

(c) What assumption was it necessary to make in order to calculate the confidence interval in **(a)**?

(d) Given that the lengths of male feet may be modelled by a normal distribution, and making any other necessary assumptions, calculate an interval within which 90% of the lengths of male feet will lie.

(e) In the light of your calculations in **(a)** and **(d)**, discuss briefly, the question 'Is a foot a foot long?' (One foot is 30.5 cm.)   [A]

Solution

(a) 95% confidence interval for mean length of male feet is

$$29.2 \pm 1.96 \times \frac{1.47}{\sqrt{180}}$$

i.e. 29.2 ± 0.215 or 28.99 to 29.41

(b) It is not necessary to assume lengths are normally distributed because the central limit theorem states that the mean of a large sample from any distribution will be approximately normally distributed.

(c) To calculate the confidence interval in **(a)** we needed to assume that the sample could be treated as a random sample from the population of all male feet.

(d) 90% of male feet will lie in the interval

$$29.2 \pm 1.6449 \times 1.47$$

i.e. 29.2 ± 2.42 or 26.78 to 31.62

(e) The confidence interval calculated in **(a)** does not contain 30.5 and so it is very unlikely that the **mean** length of male feet is one foot. The interval calculated in **(d)** does contain 30.5 which indicates that some male feet are a foot long.

EXERCISE 6B

1 A telephone company selected a random sample of size 150 from those customers who had not paid their bills one month after they had been sent out. The mean amount owed by the customers in the sample was £97.50 and the standard deviation was £29.00.
Calculate a 90% confidence interval for the mean amount owed by all customers who had not paid their bills one month after they had been sent out.

2 A sample of 64 fish caught in the river Mirwell had a mean weight of 848 g with a standard deviation of 146 g. Assuming these may be regarded as a random sample of all the fish caught in the Mirwell, calculate, for the mean of this population:

(a) a 95% confidence interval,

(b) a 64% confidence interval.

3 A boat returns from a fishing trip holding 145 cod. The mean length of these cod is 74 cm and their standard deviation is 9 cm. The cod in the boat may be regarded as a random sample from a large shoal. The normal distribution may be regarded as an adequate model for the lengths of the cod in the shoal.

(a) Calculate a 95% confidence interval for the mean length of cod in the shoal.

(b) It is known that the normal distribution is not a good model for the weights of cod in a shoal. If the cod had been weighed, what difficulties, if any, would arise in calculating a confidence interval for the mean weight of cod in the shoal? Justify your answer. [A]

4 A sweet shop sells chocolates which appear, at first sight, to be identical. Of a random sample of 80 chocolates, 61 had hard centres and the rest soft centres. The chocolates are in the shape of circular discs and the diameters, in centimetres, of the 19 soft-centred chocolates were:

> 2.79 2.63 2.84 2.77 2.81 2.69 2.66 2.71 2.62 2.75
> 2.77 2.72 2.81 2.74 2.79 2.77 2.67 2.69 2.75

The mean diameter of the 61 hard-centred chocolates was 2.690 cm.

(a) If the diameters of both hard-centred and soft-centred chocolates are known to be normally distributed with standard deviation 0.042 cm, calculate a 95% confidence interval for the mean diameter of,

(i) the soft-centred chocolates,

(ii) the hard-centred chocolates.

(b) Calculate an interval within which approximately 95% of the diameters of hard-centred chocolates will lie.

(c) Discuss, briefly, how useful knowledge of the diameter of a chocolate is in determining whether it is hard- or soft-centred. [A]

6

5 Packets of baking powder have a nominal weight of 200 g. The distribution of weights is normal and the standard deviation is 10 g. Average quantity system legislation states that, if the nominal weight is 200 g,

- the average weight must be at least 200 g,
- not more than 2.5% of packages may weigh less than 191 g,
- not more than 1 in 1000 packages may weigh less than 182 g.

A random sample of 30 packages had the following weights:

218 207 214 189 211 206 203 217 183 186
219 213 207 214 203 204 195 197 213 212
188 221 217 184 186 216 198 211 216 200

(a) Calculate a 95% confidence interval for the mean weight.

(b) Assuming that the mean is at the lower limit of the interval calculated in **(a)**, what proportion of packets would weigh,

(i) less than 191 g,

(ii) less than 182 g?

(c) Discuss the suitability of the packets from the point of view of the average quantity system. A simple adjustment will change the mean weight of future packages. Changing the standard deviation is possible but very expensive. Without carrying out any further calculations, discuss any adjustments you might recommend. [A]

Worked example 6.5

Solid fuel is packed in sacks which are then weighed on scales. It is known that if the full sack weighs μ kg the weight recorded by the scales will be normally distributed with mean μ kg and standard deviation 0.36 kg.

A particular full sack was weighed four times and the weights recorded were 34.7, 34.4, 35.1 and 34.6 kg.

(a) Calculate a 95% confidence interval for the weight of this full sack.

(b) State the width of the interval calculated in **(a)**.

(c) What percentage would be associated with a confidence interval of width 0.3 kg?

(d) How many times would this full sack have to be weighed so that a 95% confidence interval for the weight would be of width 0.3 kg?

Solution

(a) $\bar{x} = 34.7$

95% confidence interval for the mean is

$$34.7 \pm 1.96 \times \frac{0.36}{\sqrt{4}}$$

i.e. 34.7 ± 0.353 or 34.35 to 35.05

(b) width of interval is $2 \times 0.353 = 0.706$

(c) $0.3 = 2z \times \dfrac{0.36}{\sqrt{4}}$

$z = 0.833$

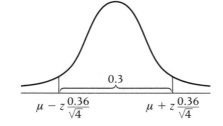

% confidence $= 100\{0.7977 - (1 - 0.7977)\}$
   i.e. 59.54 or approximately 60%.

A 60% confidence interval would have width approximately 0.3 kg.

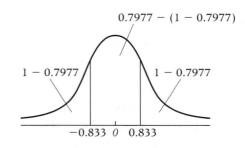

(d) $0.3 = 2 \times 1.96 \times \dfrac{0.36}{\sqrt{n}}$

$\sqrt{n} = 4.704 \qquad n = 22.1.$

If the sack was weighed 22 times a 95% confidence interval would be of width approximately 0.3 kg.

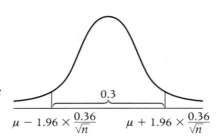

Worked example 6.6

(a) A sample of adult female bears observed in the wild had the following weights in kilograms.

   98 57 71 107   109

The data may be regarded as a random sample from a normally distributed population with a standard deviation of 11 kg.
Calculate a 99% confidence interval for the mean weight of adult female bears.

(b) A sample of adult male bears is also weighed and used to calculate both a 90% and a 95% confidence interval for μ, the mean weight of the population of adult male bears, (i.e. both confidence intervals are calculated from the same sample).

Find the probability that:

(i) the 90% confidence interval does not contain μ,

(ii) the 90% confidence interval does not contain μ but the 95% confidence interval does contain μ,

(iii) the 95% confidence interval contains μ, given that the 90% confidence interval does not contain μ,

(iv) the 90% confidence interval contains μ, given that the 95% confidence interval does not contain μ.

(c) Find the probability that the confidence interval calculated in **(a)** does not contain the mean weight of adult female bears and the 90% confidence interval in **(b)** does not contain μ. [A]

Solution

(a) $\bar{x} = 88.4$

99% confidence interval for the mean is

$$88.4 \pm 2.5758 \times \frac{11}{\sqrt{5}}$$

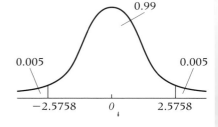

i.e 88.4 ± 12.7 or 75.7 to 101.1

(i) There is a probability of 0.9 that a 90% confidence interval contains μ and so there is a probability of $1 - 0.9 = 0.1$ that a 90% confidence interval does not contain μ.

(ii) If the 95% confidence interval contains μ but the 90% confidence interval does not contain μ then $\bar{x}$ must lie in the shaded area.

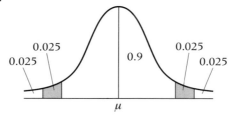

Probability is 0.05.

(iii) P(95% contains μ | 90% does not contain μ)

$$= \frac{P(95\% \text{ contains } \mu \text{ and } 90\% \text{ does not contain } \mu)}{P(90\% \text{ does not contain } \mu)}$$

$$= \frac{0.05}{0.1} = 0.5.$$

(iv) If the 95% confidence interval does not contain μ it is impossible for the 90% confidence interval to contain μ.

The probability is 0.

(c) The probability that the 99% confidence interval calculated in **(a)** does not contain the mean weight of female bears is $1 - 0.99 = 0.01$.

The probability the 90% confidence interval calculated in **(b)** does not contain μ is $1 - 0.9 = 0.1$.

Assuming that these two samples are independent the required probability is $0.01 \times 0.1 = 0.001$.

EXERCISE 6C

1 A random sample of experimental components for use in aircraft engines was tested to destruction under extreme conditions. The survival times, X days, of ten components were as follows:

207   381   111   673   234   294   897   144   418   554

(a) Assuming that the survival time, under these conditions, for all the experimental components is normally distributed with standard deviation 240 days, calculate a 90% confidence interval for the mean of X.

(b) State the probability that the confidence interval calculated in **(a)** does not contain the mean of X.

2 A car manufacturer purchases large quantities of a particular component. The working lives of the components are known to be normally distributed with mean 2400 hours and standard deviation 650 hours. The manufacturer is concerned about the large variability and the supplier undertakes to improve the design so that the standard deviation is reduced to 300 hours.

A random sample of five of the new components is tested and found to last

2730   3120   2980   2680   2800 hours.

Assuming that the lives of the new components are normally distributed with standard deviation 300 hours:

(a) **(i)** Calculate a 90% confidence interval for their mean working life.

   (ii) How many of the new components would it be necessary to test in order to make the width of a 95% confidence interval for the mean just less than 100 hours?

(b) Lives of components commonly follow a distribution which is not normal. If the assumption of normality is invalid, comment briefly on the amount of uncertainty in your answers to **(a)(i)** and **(ii)**.

(c) Is there any reason to doubt the assumption that the standard deviation of the lives of the new components is 300 hours?   [A]

6

3 A supermarket sells cartons of tea bags. The weight, in grams, of the contents of the cartons in any batch is known to be normally distributed with mean μ_T and standard deviation 4. In order to compare the actual contents with that claimed by the supplier, a manager weighed the contents of a random sample of five cartons from a large batch and obtained the following results, in grams:

> 196 202 198 197 190

(a) Calculate:
  (i) a 95% confidence interval for μ_T,
  (ii) a 60% confidence interval for μ_T.

The manager intends to do the same thing tomorrow (i.e. to weigh the contents of a random sample of cartons of tea and to use the data collected to calculate both a 95% and a 60% confidence interval).

(b) State the probability that:
  (i) the 95% confidence interval she calculates will not contain μ_T,
  (ii) neither of the confidence intervals she calculates will contain μ_T.

The manager also intends to weigh the contents of jars of coffee from a batch in order to calculate a 95% and a 60% confidence interval for the mean contents, μ_C, of jars in the batch. However, in this case, the 95% confidence interval will be calculated from one random sample and the 60% confidence interval calculated from a second, independent, random sample.

(c) Find the probability that neither the 60% nor the 95% confidence interval for the mean contents of jars of coffee will contain μ_C. [A]

4 Batteries supplied to a large institution for use in electric clocks had a mean working life of 960 days with a standard deviation of 135 days.

A sample from a new supplier had working lives of

> 1020, 998, 894, 921, 843, 1280, 1302, 782, 694, 1350 days.

Assume that the data may be regarded as a random sample from a normal distribution with standard deviation 135 days.

(a) For the working lives of batteries from the new supplier, calculate a 95% confidence interval for the mean.

(b) The institution would like batteries with a large mean. Compare the two sources of supply.

(c) State the width of the confidence interval calculated in **(a)**.

(d) What percentage would be associated with an interval of width 100 days calculated from the data above?

(e) How large a sample would be needed to calculate a 90% confidence interval of width approximately 100 days? [A]

Key point summary

1 If $\bar{x}$ is the mean of a random sample of size n from a   *p109*
normal distribution with (unknown) mean μ and
(known) standard deviation σ, a $100(1 - \alpha)\%$
confidence interval for μ is given by $\bar{x} \pm z_{\frac{\alpha}{2}} \dfrac{\sigma}{\sqrt{n}}$.

2 If a large random sample is available: *p113*

- it can be used to provide a good estimate of
  the population standard deviation σ,

- it is safe to assume that the mean is normally distributed.

Test yourself   What to review

1 The lengths of components produced by a machine are   *Section 6.2*
normally distributed with standard deviation 0.005 cm.
A random sample of components measured

     1.002   1.007   1.016   1.009   1.003 cm.

Calculate a 95% confidence interval for the population mean.

---

2 State the probability that an 85% confidence interval for μ *Section 6.2*
does not contain μ.

---

3 The contents of a random sample of 80 tins of vindaloo cooking   *Section 6.3*
sauce from a large batch were weighed. The sample mean
content was 284.2 g and the standard deviation, s, was found
to be 4.1 g.

Calculate a 95% confidence interval for the population mean.

---

4 How would your answer to question 3 be affected if it was   *Section 6.3*
later discovered that the batch contained tins which had been
produced on two different machines and the distribution of
the weights was bimodal?

---

5 How would your answer to question 3 be affected if it was   *Section 6.3*
later discovered that the sample was not random?

Test yourself   ANSWERS

5 If the sample was not random this would make the confidence interval
unreliable. For example, the sample of tins could all have come from
the same machine leading to a biased result.

4 It would not affect the answer. The sample is stated to be a random
sample from the whole batch and the central limit theorem applies to
all distributions whether bimodal or not.

1 1.0030–1.0118.   **2** 0.15.   **3** 283.30–285.10.

CHAPTER 7

Hypothesis testing

Learning objectives

After studying this chapter you should be able to:
- define a null and alternative hypothesis
- define the significance level of a hypothesis test
- identify a critical region
- understand whether to use a one- or a two-tailed test
- understand what is meant by a **Type 1** and a **Type 2** error
- test a hypothesis about a population mean based on a sample from a normal distribution with known standard deviation
- test a hypothesis about a population mean based on a large sample.

7.1 Forming a hypothesis

One of the most important applications of statistics is to use a *sample* to test an idea, or hypothesis, you have regarding a population. This is one of the methods of statistical inference referred to in section 6.1.

Conclusions can never be absolutely certain but the risk of your conclusion being incorrect can be quantified (measured) and can enable you to identify *statistically significant* results.

> Statistically significant results require overwhelming evidence.

In any experiment, you will have your own idea or hypothesis as to how you expect the results to turn out.

A **Null Hypothesis**, written H_0, is set up at the start of any hypothesis test. This null hypothesis is a statement which defines the population and so always contains '=' signs, never '>', '<' or '≠'.

An example of a Null Hypothesis which you will meet in Worked example 7.1 is:

H_0 Population mean lifetime of bulbs, $\mu = 500$ hours.

Usually, you are hoping to show that the Null Hypothesis is **not** true and so the **Alternative Hypothesis**, written H_1, is often the hypothesis you want to establish. Worked example 7.1 has:

H_1 Population mean lifetime of bulbs, $\mu > 500$ hours.

> The **null hypothesis** is only abandoned in the face of overwhelming evidence that it cannot explain the experimental results.
> Rather like in a court of law where the defendant is considered innocent until the evidence proves without doubt that he or she is guilty, the H_0 is accepted as true until test results show overwhelmingly that they cannot be explained if it was true.

> It often seems strange to students that they may want to show that H_0 is **not** true but, considering the examples of H_0 and H_1 given here, a manufacturer may well hope to show that bulbs have a **longer** than average lifetime.

A hypothesis test needs two hypotheses identified at the beginning: H_0 the **Null Hypothesis** and H_1 the **Alternative Hypothesis**.

H_0 states that a situation is unchanged, that a population parameter takes its usual value.
H_1 states that the parameter has increased, decreased or just changed.

7.2 One- and two-tailed tests

Tests which involve an H_1 with a $>$ or $<$ sign are called **one-tailed** tests because we are expecting to find just an increase or just a decrease.

Tests which involve an H_1 with a $\neq$ sign are called **two-tailed** tests as they consider any change (whether it be an increase or decrease).

For example, if data were collected on the amount of weekly pocket money given to a random selection of children aged between 12 and 14 in a rural area, and also in a city, it may be that you are interested in investigating whether children in the city are given **more** pocket money than children in rural areas. Therefore, you may set up your hypotheses as:

H_0 Average pocket money of children is the same in the rural area and in the city, or

$\qquad \mu \,(\text{city}) = \mu \,(\text{rural})$

H_1 Average pocket money **greater** in city, or

$\qquad \mu \,(\text{city}) > \mu \,(\text{rural})$

This is an example of a **one-tailed** test.

However, if you were monitoring the weight of items produced in a factory, it would be likely that **any** change, be it an increase or decrease, would be a problem and there would not necessarily be any reason to expect a change of a specific type.
In this case, typical hypotheses would be:

H_0 Population mean weight is 35 g

$\qquad \mu = 35 \text{ g}$

H_1 Population mean weight **is not** 35 g

$\qquad \mu \neq 35 \text{ g}$

This is an example of a **two-tailed** test.

One-tailed tests will generally involve words such as:
better or worse,
faster or slower,
more or less,
bigger or smaller,
increase or decrease.
In Worked example 7.1,
H_1 $\mu > 500$ hours indicates a **one-tailed** test.

Two-tailed tests will generally involve words such as:
different or difference,
change,
affected.

A **two-tailed** test is one where H_1 involves testing for any (non-directional) change in a parameter.
A **one-tailed** test is one where H_1 involves testing specifically for an increase or for a decrease (change in one direction only).

7.3 Testing a hypothesis about a population mean

Carrying out a hypothesis test to determine whether a population mean is significantly different from the suggested value stated in H_0 involves calculating a **test statistic** from a sample taken from the population.

As the test involves the population mean, it is the **sample mean**, $\bar{x}$, which must be evaluated. Since this test concerns a sample taken from a *normal* distribution, we also know that the sample means follow a normal distribution with mean equal to μ and with standard deviation equal to $\frac{\sigma}{\sqrt{n}}$.

The **test statistic** simply standardises the sample mean, $\bar{x}$, so that the result can be compared to critical z-values.

It is very important that it can be assumed or known that the sample has been selected **randomly.** If the sample were not selected randomly, then valid conclusions regarding the whole population cannot be made since the sample may only represent one part of that population.

7

Test statistic $= \dfrac{\bar{x} - \mu}{\dfrac{\sigma}{\sqrt{n}}}$

7.4 Critical region and significance level of test

The **critical region** is the range of values of the test statistic which is so unlikely to occur when H_0 is true, that it will lead to the conclusion that H_0 is not true. The **significance level** of a test determines what is considered the level of overwhelming evidence necessary for the decision to conclude that H_0 is not true. It is the probability of wrongly rejecting a true H_0. The smaller the significance level, the more overwhelming the evidence required. Common values used for **significance levels** are 1%, 5% or 10%.

The test introduced in this chapter is based on a sample from a normal distribution. Therefore, the **critical region** is identified by finding critical z-values from Table 4, 'Percentage

Table 4 is in the AQA Formulae book and in the Appendix.

points of the normal distribution', in exactly the same way as the z-values were found in order for confidence intervals to be constructed.

See chapter 6.

Some examples of critical regions are illustrated below.

One-tailed tests at 5% significance level

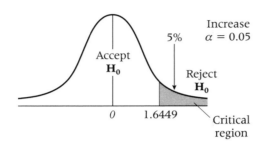

A 5% significance level is denoted $\alpha = 0.05$.

$z_\alpha = 1.6449$.

$z_\alpha = -1.6449$.

One-tailed tests at 1% significance level

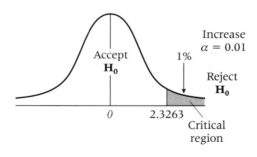

A 1% significance level is denoted $\alpha = 0.01$.

$z_\alpha = 2.3263$.

$z_\alpha = -2.3263$.

Two-tailed tests at 5% and 10% significance levels

Two critical values – change at both ends is considered.

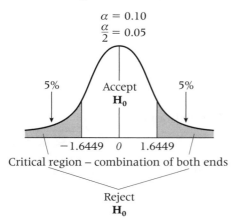

$\alpha = 0.10$
$\frac{\alpha}{2} = 0.05$

Critical region – combination of both ends

$z_{\frac{\alpha}{2}} = \pm 1.6449 \quad \alpha = 0.10.$

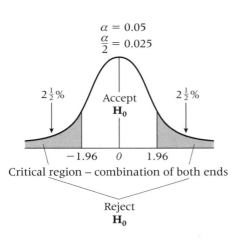

$\alpha = 0.05$
$\frac{\alpha}{2} = 0.025$

Critical region – combination of both ends

$z_{\frac{\alpha}{2}} = \pm 1.96 \quad \alpha = 0.05.$

7

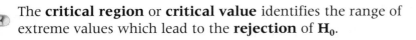

> The **critical region** or **critical value** identifies the range of extreme values which lead to the **rejection** of H_0.

> The **significance level**, α, of a test is the probability that a test statistic lies in the extreme critical region, if H_0 is true. It determines the level of overwhelming evidence deemed necessary for the rejection of H_0.

7.5 General procedure for carrying out a hypothesis test

> The general procedure for hypothesis testing is:
> 1 Write down H_0 and H_1 4 Identify the critical region
> 2 Decide which test to use   5 Calculate the test statistic
> 3 Decide on the significance level   6 Draw your conclusion

Worked example 7.1

The lifetimes (hours) of Xtralong light bulbs are known to be normally distributed with a standard deviation of 90 hours.

A random sample of ten light bulbs is taken from a large batch produced in the Xtralong factory after an expensive machinery overhaul.

The lifetimes of these bulbs were measured as

    523 556 678 429 558 498 399 515 555 699 hours.

Before the overhaul the mean life was 500 hours.

Investigate, at the 5% significance level, whether the mean life of Xtralong light bulbs has increased after the overhaul.

> The bulbs may appear to have a longer mean lifetime now but this may not be statistically significant.

Solution

The important facts to note are:

We are testing whether the mean is still 500 hours or whether an increase has occurred.

This means that $\mathbf{H_0}$ is $\mu = 500$ hours
          and $\mathbf{H_1}$ is $\mu > 500$ hours a **one-tailed** test.

The test is at the **5%** significance level.

The lifetimes are normally distributed with known standard deviation of 90 hours.

The hypothesis test is carried out as follows:

$\mathbf{H_0}$ $\mu = 500$ hours
$\mathbf{H_1}$ $\mu > 500$ hours $\alpha = 0.05$

From tables, the critical value is z = 1.6449 for this one-tailed test.

The sample mean, $\bar{x} = 541$ hours, from a sample with $n = 10$.

The population standard deviation is known, $\sigma = 90$ hours.

Therefore the test statistic

$$\frac{\bar{x} - \mu}{\frac{\sigma}{\sqrt{n}}} = \frac{541 - 500}{\frac{90}{\sqrt{10}}} = 1.44$$

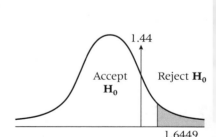

Conclusion

1.44 < 1.6449 for this one-tailed test, hence $\mathbf{H_0}$ is accepted.

There is no significant evidence to suggest that an increase in mean lifetime has occurred since the overhaul.

> Notice that we have not **proved** that $\mu = 500$ hours but we have shown that if $\mu = 500$ hours, a sample mean of 541 is not a particularly unlikely event.

Worked example 7.2

A forestry worker decided to keep records of the first year's growth of pine seedlings. Over several years, she found that the growth followed a normal distribution with a mean of 11.5 cm and a standard deviation of 2.5 cm.

Last year, she used an experimental soil preparation for the pine seedlings and the first year's growth of a sample of eight of the seedlings was

  7   22   19   15   11   18   17   15 cm.

Investigate, at the 1% significance level, whether there has been a change in the mean growth. Assume the standard deviation has not changed.

Solution

The important facts to note are:

We are testing whether the mean is 11.5 cm or not.

This means that $\mathbf{H_0}$ is $\mu = 11.5$ cm
      and $\mathbf{H_1}$ is $\mu \neq 11.5$ cm a **two-tailed** test.

The test is at the **1%** significance level.

The growth is normally distributed with known standard deviation of 2.5 cm.

The hypothesis test is carried out as follows:

   $\mathbf{H_0}\ \mu = 11.5$ cm
   $\mathbf{H_1}\ \mu \neq 11.5$ cm $\alpha = 0.01$

From tables, the critical values are $z_{\frac{\alpha}{2}} = \pm 2.5758$ for this two-tailed test.

The sample mean, $\bar{x} = 15.5$, from a sample with $n = 8$.

The population standard deviation is known, $\sigma = 2.5$ cm.

Therefore the test statistic
$$\frac{\bar{x} - \mu}{\frac{\sigma}{\sqrt{n}}} = \frac{15.5 - 11.5}{\frac{2.5}{\sqrt{8}}} = 4.53$$

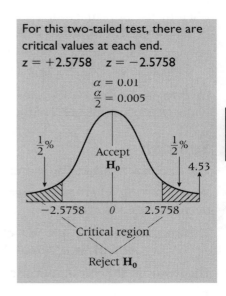

For this two-tailed test, there are critical values at each end.
$z = +2.5758 \quad z = -2.5758$

$\alpha = 0.01$
$\dfrac{\alpha}{2} = 0.005$

$\frac{1}{2}\%$ Accept $\frac{1}{2}\%$
         $\mathbf{H_0}$ 4.53

-2.5758 0   2.5758

Critical region

Reject $\mathbf{H_0}$

Conclusion

4.53 > 2.5758 for this two-tailed test, hence $\mathbf{H_0}$ is clearly rejected.

There is significant evidence to suggest that a change in mean growth has occurred.

It is clear from the data that the mean has **increased**. You can conclude that the mean has **changed** or that it has **increased**. Either would be accepted in an examination.

Worked example 7.3

The owner of a small vineyard has an old bottling machine which is used for filling bottles with his wine. The bottles contain a nominal 75 cl of wine.

The old machine is known to dispense volumes of wine which are normally distributed with mean 76.4 cl and a standard deviation of 0.9 cl.

The owner is concerned that his old machine is becoming unreliable and he decides to purchase a new bottling machine. The manufacturer assures the owner that the new machine will dispense volumes which are normally distributed with a standard deviation of 0.9 cl.

The owner wishes to reduce the mean volume dispensed.

A random sample of twelve 75 cl bottles are taken from a batch filled by the new machine and the volume of wine in each bottle is measured. The volumes were

    75.7 76.2 75.4 75.8 75.4 76.9
    76.4 75.5 76.1 76.8 76.7 76.5 cl.

Investigate, at the 5% significance level, whether the volume of wine dispensed has been reduced.

Solution

The important facts to note are:

We are testing whether the mean is still 76.4 cl or whether a decrease has occurred.

This means that $\mathbf{H_0}$ is $\mu = 76.4$ cl
          and $\mathbf{H_1}$ is $\mu < 76.4$ cl a **one-tailed** test.

The test is at the **5%** significance level.

The volumes are normally distributed with known standard deviation of 0.9 cl.

The hypothesis test is carried out as follows:

    $\mathbf{H_0}\ \mu = 76.4$ cl
    $\mathbf{H_1}\ \mu < 76.4$ cl $\alpha = 0.05$

From tables, the critical value is $z = -1.6449$ for this one-tailed test.

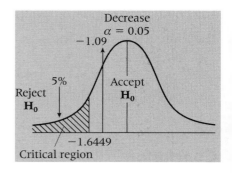

The sample mean, $\bar{x} = 76.116\,67$ cl, from a sample with $n = 12$.

The population standard deviation is known, $\sigma = 0.9$ cl.

Therefore the test statistic

$$\frac{\bar{x} - \mu}{\dfrac{\sigma}{\sqrt{n}}} = \frac{76.116\,67 - 76.4}{\dfrac{0.9}{\sqrt{12}}} = -1.09$$

Conclusion

$-1.09 > -1.6449$ for this one-tailed test, hence $\mathbf{H_0}$ is accepted.

There is no significant evidence to suggest that the mean volume has decreased.

EXERCISE 7A

1 A factory produces lengths of rope for use in boatyards. The breaking strengths of these lengths of rope follow a normal distribution with a standard deviation of 4 kg.
The breaking strengths, in kg, of a random sample of 14 lengths of rope were as follows:

      134   136   139   143   136   129   137
      130   138   134   145   141   136   139.

The lengths of rope are intended to have a breaking strength of 135 kg but the manufacturer claims that the mean breaking strength is in fact greater than 135 kg.
Investigate the manufacturer's claim using a 5% level of significance.

2 Reaction times of adults in a controlled laboratory experiment are normally distributed with a standard deviation of 5 s.
Twenty-five adults were selected at random to take part in such an experiment and the following reaction times, in seconds, were recorded:

      6.5   3.4   5.6   6.9   7.1   4.9   10.9   7.8
      2.4   2.8   11.3   3.7   7.8   2.4   2.8   3.7
      4.9   12.0   6.5   12.8   6.9   7.4   3.1   1.9   11.5

Investigate, using a 5% significance level, the hypothesis that the mean reaction time of adults is 7.5 s.

3 A maze is devised and after many trials, it is found that the length of time taken by adults to solve the maze is normally distributed with mean 7.4 s and standard deviation 2.2 s.
A group of nine children was randomly selected and asked to attempt the maze. Their times, in seconds, to completion were:

      6.1   9.0   8.3   9.4   5.8   8.1   7.6   9.2   10.0

Assuming that the times for children are also normally distributed with a standard deviation of 2.2 s, investigate, using the 5% significance level, whether children take longer than adults to do the maze.

4 A machine produces steel rods which are supposed to be of length 2 cm. The lengths of these rods are normally distributed with a standard deviation of 0.02 cm.
A random sample of ten rods is taken from the production line and their lengths measured. The lengths are:

      1.99 1.98 1.96 1.97 1.99 1.96 2.0 1.97 1.95 2.01 cm.

Investigate, at the 1% significance level, whether the mean length of rods is satisfactory.

5   The resistances, in ohms, of pieces of silver wire follow a
    normal distribution with a standard deviation of 0.02.
    A random sample of nine pieces of wire are taken from a batch
    and their resistances were measured with results:

    1.53 1.48 1.51 1.48 1.54 1.52 1.54 1.49 1.51 .

    It is known that, if the wire is pure silver, the resistance
    should be 1.50 ohms but, if the wire is impure, the resistance
    will be increased.
    Investigate, at the 5% significance level, whether the batch
    contains pure silver wire.

6   The weight of Venus chocolate bars is normally distributed
    with a mean of 30 g and a standard deviation of 3.5 g.
    A random sample of 20 Venus bars was taken from the
    production line and was found to have a mean of 32.5 g. Is
    there evidence, at the 1% significance level, that the mean
    weight has increased?

7   The weights of components produced by a certain machine are
    normally distributed with mean 15.4 g and standard deviation
    2.3 g.
    The setting on the machine is altered and, following this, a
    random sample of 81 components is found to have a mean
    weight of 15.0 g.
    Does this provide evidence, at the 5% level, of a reduction in
    the mean weight of components produced by the machine?
    Assume that the standard deviation remains unaltered.

8   The ability to withstand pain is known to vary from individual
    to individual.
    In a standard test, a tiny electric shock is applied to the finger
    until a tingling sensation is felt. When this test was applied to
    a random sample of ten adults, the times recorded, in seconds,
    before they experienced a tingling sensation were:

    4.2 4.5 3.9 4.4 4.1 4.5 3.7 4.8 4.2 4.2

    Test, at the 5% level, the hypothesis that the mean time before
    an adult would experience a tingling sensation is 4.0 s. The
    times are known to be normally distributed with a standard
    deviation of 0.2 s.

7.6 Significance levels and problems to consider

You may have wondered how the **significance level** used in
hypothesis testing is chosen. You have read that significance
levels commonly used are 1%, 5% or 10% but no explanation has
been offered about why this is so.

A common question asked by students is:

> *Why is the level of overwhelming evidence necessary to lead to rejection of H_0 commonly set at 5% ?*

The **significance level** of a hypothesis test gives the P(test statistic lies inside critical region | H_0 true).
In other words, *if* H_0 is true, then, with a 5% significance level, you would expect a result as extreme as this only once in every 20 times. If the test statistic does lie in the critical region the result is statistically significant at the 5% level and we conclude that H_0 is **untrue**.

Sometimes it may be necessary to be 'more certain' of a conclusion. If a traditional trusted piece of research is to be challenged, then a 1% level of significance may be used to ensure greater confidence in rejecting H_0.
If a new drug is to be used in preference to a well-known one then a 0.1% level may be necessary to ensure that no chance or fluke effects occur in research which leads to conclusions which may affect human health.

7.7 Errors

It is often quite a surprising concept for students to realise that, having correctly carried out a hypothesis test on carefully collected data and having made the relevant conclusion to accept the H_0 as true or to reject it as false, this conclusion might be right or it might be wrong.
However, you can never be absolutely certain that your conclusion is correct and has not occurred because of a *freak* result.
The significance level identifies for you the risk of a freak result leading to a wrong decision to reject H_0.
This leads many students to ask why tests so often use a **5% significance level** which has a probability of 0.05 of incorrectly rejecting H_0 when it actually is true. Why not reduce the significance level to 0.1% and then there would be a negligible risk of 0.001 of this error occurring?

The answer to this question comes from considering the **two** errors which may occur when conducting a hypothesis test. This table illustrates the problems:

7

		Conclusion	
		H_0 true	H_0 not true
Reality	H_0 correct	Conclusion correct	Error made **Type 1**
	H_0 incorrect	Error made **Type 2**	Conclusion correct

Not only can you conclude H_0 is true when really it is false but also you could conclude it is false when actually it is true.

The table shows that the **significance level** of a test is
P(conclusion H_0 not true | H_0 really is correct) =
P(**Type 1** error made).

The other error to consider is when a test does not show a
significant result even though the H_0 actually is **not** true.
P(conclusion H_0 true | H_0 really is incorrect)
= P(**Type 2** error made).

The probability of making a **Type 2** error is difficult or
impossible to evaluate unless precise further information is
available about values of the population parameters. If a value
suggested in H_0 is only slightly incorrect then there may be a
very high probability of making a **Type 2** error. If the value is
completely incorrect then the probability of a **Type 2** error will
be very small.

> You will not be expected to evaluate the probability of making a **Type 2** error in S5.

Obviously, if you set a very low **significance level** for a test,
then the probability of making a **Type 1** error will be low but
you may well have quite a high probability of making a **Type 2**
error.

There is no logical reason why 5% is used, rather than 4% or 6%.
However, practical experience over a long period of time has
shown that, in most circumstances, a significance level of 5%
gives a good balance between the risks of making **Type 1** and
Type 2 errors.

> If a low risk of wrongly rejecting H_0 is set, then it is unlikely that the test statistic will lie in the critical region. H_0 is unlikely to be rejected unless the null hypothesis is 'miles away' from reality.

This is why 5% is chosen as the 'standard' significance level for
hypothesis testing and careful consideration must be given
before changing this value.

> Errors which can occcur are:
> A **Type 1** error which is to reject H_0 when it is true.
> A **Type 2** error which is to accept H_0 when it is not true.

Worked example 7.4

A set of times, measured to one-hundredth of a second, were
obtained from nine randomly selected subjects taking part in a
psychology experiment.

The mean of the nine sample times was found to be 9.17 s.

It is known that these times are normally distributed with a
standard deviation of 4.25 s.

The hypothesis that the mean of such times is equal to 7.50 s is
to be tested, with an alternative hypothesis that the mean is
greater than 7.50 s, using a 5% level of significance.

Explain, in the context of this situation, the meaning of:

(a) a **Type 1** error,
(b) a **Type 2** error.

Solution

For this example:

$\mathbf{H_0}$ $\mu = 7.50$ s
$\mathbf{H_1}$ $\mu > 7.50$ s $\alpha = 0.05$ one-tailed test.

(a) A **Type 1** error is to reject $\mathbf{H_0}$ and conclude that the population mean time is **greater than** 7.50 s when, in reality, the mean time for such an experiment is equal to 7.50 s.

> If $\mathbf{H_0}$ is untrue it is impossible to make a **Type 1** error.

The probability of this happening, if $\mathbf{H_0}$ is true is $\alpha = 0.05$.

(b) A **Type 2** error is to accept $\mathbf{H_0}$ and conclude that the population mean time is **equal to** 7.50 s when, in reality, the mean time for such an experiment is greater than 7.50 s.

> If $\mathbf{H_0}$ is true it is impossible to make a **Type 2** error.

The probability of this happening will vary and can only be determined if more information is given regarding the exact alternative value that μ may take, not simply that $\mu > 7.50$ s.

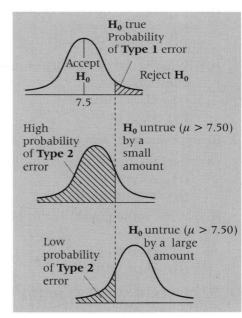

7

Worked example 7.5

Explain, in the context of Worked example 7.2, the meaning of:

(a) a **Type 1** error,
(b) a **Type 2** error.

Solution

In Worked example 7.2, we have:

$\mathbf{H_0}$ $\mu = 11.5$ cm
$\mathbf{H_1}$ $\mu \neq 11.5$ cm $\alpha = 0.01$

Hence:

(a) A **Type 1** error is to reject H_0 and conclude that the mean growth of seedlings is **not equal** to 11.5 cm when, in reality, the mean growth for seedlings grown in the experimental soil preparation is equal to 11.5 cm.

The probability of this happening if H_0 is true is $\alpha = 0.01$.

(b) A **Type 2** error is to accept H_0 and conclude that the mean growth of seedlings is **equal** to 11.5 cm when, in reality, the mean growth for the seedlings grown in the experimental soil preparation is not equal to 11.5 cm.

As seen in the previous example, the probability of this cannot be determined unless precise information is given regarding the alternative value taken by μ.

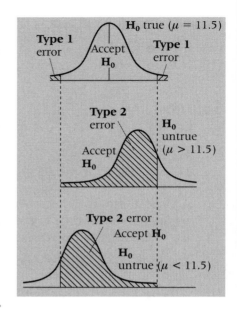

EXERCISE 7B

1 Refer to question **1** in exercise 7A.

   (a) Explain, in the context of this question, the meaning of:
      (i) a **Type 1** error,
      (ii) a **Type 2** error.

   (b) What is the probability of making a **Type 1** error in this question if:
      (i) H_0 is true,
      (ii) H_0 is untrue?

2 Refer to question **4** in exercise 7A.

   (a) Explain, in the context of this question, the meaning of:
      (i) a **Type 1** error,
      (ii) a **Type 2** error.

   (b) What is the probability of making a **Type 1** error in this question if:
      (i) H_0 is true,
      (ii) H_0 is untrue?

3 Times for glaze to set on pottery bowls follow a normal distribution with a standard deviation of three minutes. The mean time is believed to be 20 minutes.
A random sample of nine bowls is glazed with times which gave a sample mean of 18.2 minutes.

   (a) Investigate, at the 5% significance level, whether the results of this sample support the belief that the mean glaze time is 20 minutes.

   (b) Explain, in the context of this question, the meaning of a **Type 1** error.

   (c) Why is it not possible to find the probability that a **Type 2** error is made?

4 The lengths of car components are normally distributed with a standard deviation of 0.45 mm. Ten components are selected at random from a large batch and their lengths were found to be,

     19.3 20.5 18.1 18.3 17.6 19.0 20.1 19.2 18.6 19.4 mm.

(a) Investigate, at the 10% significance level, the claim that the mean length of such components is 19.25 mm.

(b) Explain, in the context of this question, the meaning of:
  (i) a **Type 1** error,
  (ii) a **Type 2** error.

(c) Write down the probability of making a **Type 1** error if the mean length is 19.25 mm.

5 A random sample of ten assembly workers in a large factory are trained and then asked to assemble a new design of electrical appliance. The times to assemble this appliance are known to follow a normal distribution with a standard deviation of 12 minutes. It is claimed that the new design is easier to assemble and the mean time should be less than the mean of 47 minutes currently taken to assemble the old design of appliance.
The mean time for the sample of ten workers was 39.8 minutes.

(a) Investigate, using a 5% significance level, the claim that the new design is easier to assemble.

(b) Explain, in the context of this question, the meaning of a **Type 2** error.

7

7.8 Hypothesis test for means based on a large sample from an unspecified distribution

As discussed in section 6.3, there are occasionally real life situations where we may wish to carry out a hypothesis test for a mean by examining a sample taken from a population where the standard deviation is known. However, it is much more likely that, if the mean of the population is unknown, the standard deviation will also be unknown. Provided that a large sample is available, then a sufficiently good estimate of the population standard deviation can be found from the sample. The use of a large sample also has the advantage that the sample mean is approximately normally distributed regardless of the distribution of the population.

> The definition of large is arbitrary but a sample size of $n \geqslant 30$ is usually considered 'large'.

> It is still important to ensure that the sample is randomly selected.

As in section 6.3, the **sample mean**, $\bar{x}$, is evaluated and, since this test involves a **large** sample, we know that the sample mean is approximately normally distributed. The standard deviation is also evaluated and used as an estimate of σ for this test.

> As the sample is large it makes very little difference whether the divisor n or $n - 1$ is used when estimating σ. However as σ is being estimated from a sample it is correct to use the divisor $n - 1$.

The **test statistic** is $\dfrac{\bar{x} - \mu}{\dfrac{\sigma}{\sqrt{n}}}$ as before, and is compared to critical z-values.

To carry out a hypothesis test for a mean based on a **large** sample from an **unspecified** distribution:

the **test statistic** is $\dfrac{\bar{x} - \mu}{\frac{\sigma}{\sqrt{n}}}$.

An estimate of the standard deviation, σ, can be made from the sample, the **test statistic** is compared to **critical z-values**. These are found in AQA Table 4, in the Appendix.

Worked example 7.6

A manufacturer claims that the mean lifetime of her batteries is 425 hours. A competitor tests a random sample of 250 of these batteries and the mean lifetime is found to be 408 hours, with a standard deviation of 68 hours.

Investigate the claim of the competitor that the batteries have a mean lifetime less than 425 hours. Use a 1% significance level.

Solution

The important facts to note are:

We are testing whether the population mean lifetime is 425 hours or whether it is less than 425 hours.

This means that $\mathbf{H_0}$ is $\mu = 425$ hours
and $\mathbf{H_1}$ is $\mu < 425$ hours a **one-tailed** test.

The test is at the **1%** significance level.

The lifetimes are from an unspecified distribution with an unknown standard deviation. However, the sample size is **large** so $\bar{x}$ is approximately normally distributed and an estimate of the unknown population standard deviation can be calculated from the sample.

$n = 250.$

The hypothesis test is carried out as follows:

$\mathbf{H_0}$ $\mu = 425$ hours
$\mathbf{H_1}$ $\mu < 425$ hours $\quad \alpha = 0.01$

From tables, the critical value is $z = -2.3263$ for this one-tailed test.

The sample mean, $\bar{x} = 408$ hours, from a sample with $n = 250$.

The population standard deviation is estimated as $\sigma = 68$ hours.

The **test statistic** is $\dfrac{\bar{x} - \mu}{\frac{\sigma}{\sqrt{n}}} = \dfrac{408 - 425}{\frac{68}{\sqrt{250}}} = -3.95$

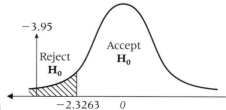

Conclusion

$-3.95 < -2.3263$ for this one-tailed test. Hence $\mathbf{H_0}$ is rejected.

There is significant evidence to suggest that the mean lifetime is less than the 425 hours claimed by the manufacturer.

Worked example 7.7

A precision machine is set to produce metal rods which have a mean length of 2 mm. A sample of 150 of these rods is randomly selected from the production of this machine. The sample mean is 1.97 mm and the standard deviation is 0.28 mm.

(a) Investigate, using the 5% significance level, the claim that the mean length of rods produced by the machine is 2 mm.

(b) How would your conclusions be affected if you later discovered that:

    (i) the sample was not random,

    (ii) the distribution was not normal?   [A]

Solution

(a) The important facts to note are:

We are testing whether or not the population mean length is 2 mm.

This is a **two-tailed** test.
The test is at the **5%** significance level.
The lengths are from an unspecified distribution with an unknown standard deviation. However, the sample size is **large**.
The hypothesis test is carried out as follows:

$$\mathbf{H_0}\ \mu = 2\ \text{mm}$$
$$\mathbf{H_1}\ \mu \neq 2\ \text{mm} \quad \alpha = 0.05$$

From tables, the critical value is $z = \pm 1.96$ for this two-tailed test.
The sample mean, $\bar{x} = 1.97$ mm, from a sample with $n = 150$.
The population standard deviation is estimated as $\sigma = 0.28$ mm.

The **test statistic** is $\dfrac{\bar{x} - \mu}{\dfrac{\sigma}{\sqrt{n}}} = \dfrac{1.97 - 2}{\dfrac{0.28}{\sqrt{150}}} = -1.31$

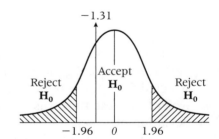

Conclusion

$-1.31 > -1.96$ for this two-tailed test. Hence $\mathbf{H_0}$ is accepted.

There is no significant evidence to suggest that a change in mean length has occurred.

We have shown that if $\mu = 2$ mm, a sample mean of 1.97 is not a particularly unlikely event.

(b) **(i)** If the sample was not random there can be no confidence in the conclusion. For example, these may have been the first 150 rods produced and the mean length could have changed as production continued.

    (ii) It makes no difference whether the distribution is normal or not as this is a large sample.

EXERCISE 7C

1 A factory produces lengths of cable for use in winches. These lengths are intended to have a mean breaking strength of 195 kg but the factory claims that the mean breaking strength is in fact greater than 195 kg.
In order to investigate this claim, a random sample of 80 lengths of cable is checked. The breaking strengths of these sample lengths are found to have a mean of 199.7 kg and a standard deviation of 17.4 kg. Carry out a suitable hypothesis test, using a 1% level of significance, to test the factory's claim.

2 The resistances of 5 mm pieces of wire for use in an electronics factory are supposed to have a mean of 1.5.
A random sample of 85 pieces of wire are taken from a large delivery and their resistances are carefully measured. Their mean resistance is 1.6 ohms and their standard deviation is 0.9 ohms.
Investigate, at the 5% significance level, whether the mean resistance is 1.5 ohms.

3 A Government department states that the mean score of Year 2 children in a new national assessment test is 78%.
A large education authority selected 90 Year 2 children at random from all those who took this test in their area and found that the mean score for these children was 72.8%, with a standard deviation of 18.5%.
Investigate, using a 5% significance level, the hypothesis that the mean score of children in this area is lower than 78%.

4 A large dairy company produces whipped spread which is packaged into 500 g plastic tubs. Sixty tubs were randomly selected from the production line and weighed. The mean weight of these tubs was found to be 504 g with a standard deviation of 17.3 g.
Investigate, using the 5% significance level, whether the mean weight of the tubs is greater than 500 g.

5 A machine produces steel rods which are supposed to be of length 30 mm. A customer suspects that the mean length of the rods is less than 30 mm. The customer selects 50 rods from a large batch and measures their lengths.
The mean length of the rods in this sample was found to be 29.1 mm with a standard deviation of 2.9 mm.
Investigate, at the 1% significance level, whether the customer's suspicions are correct.
What assumption was it necessary to make in order to carry out this test?

6 The weight of Bubbles biscuit bars is meant to have a mean of 35 g.
A random sample of 120 Bubbles bars is taken from the production line and it is found that their mean weight is 36.5 g. The standard deviation of the sample weights is 8.8 g. Is there evidence, at the 1% significance level, that the mean weight is greater than 35 g?

7 Varicoceles is a medical condition in adolescent boys which may lead to infertility. A recent edition of *The Lancet* reported a study from Italy which suggested that the presence of this condition may be detected using a surgical instrument. The instrument gives a mean reading of 7.4 for adolescent boys who do not suffer from varicoceles. A sample of 73 adolescent boys who suffered from varicoceles gave a mean reading of 6.7 and a standard deviation of 1.2.

 (a) Stating your null and alternative hypotheses and using a 5% significance level, investigate whether the mean reading for all adolescent boys who suffer from varicoceles is less than 7.4.

 (b) Making reference to the value of your test statistic, comment briefly on the strength of the conclusion you have drawn.

 (c) State, and discuss the validity of, any assumptions you have made in **(a)** about the method of sampling and about the distribution from which the data were drawn. [A]

MIXED EXERCISE

1 It is known that repeated weighings of the same object on a particular chemical balance give readings which are normally distributed.
Past evidence, using experienced operators, suggests that the mean is equal to the mass of the object and that the standard deviation is 0.25 mg. A trainee operator makes seven repeated weighings of the same object, which is known to have a mass of 19.5 mg, and obtains the following readings:

 19.1   19.4   19.0   18.8   19.7   19.8   19.2

Investigate using the 5% significance level, whether the trainee operator's readings are biased.

Assume the standard deviation for the trainee operator is 0.25 mg.

2 An investigation was conducted into the dust content in the flue gases of a particular type of solid-fuel boiler. Forty boilers were used under identical fuelling and extraction conditions. Over a given period, the quantities, in grams, of dust which was deposited in traps inserted in each of the forty flues were measured. The mean quantity for this sample of forty boilers was found to be 65.7 g, with a standard deviation of 2.9 g.

Investigate, at the 1% level of significance, the hypothesis that the population mean dust deposit is 60 g.

3 A large food processing firm is considering introducing a new recipe for its ice cream. In a preliminary trial, a panel of 15 tasters were each asked to score the ice cream on a scale from 0 (awful) to 20 (excellent). Their scores were as follows:

16 15 17 6 18 15 18 7 4 16 12 14 6 17 11

The scores in a similar trial for the firm's existing ice cream were normally distributed with mean 14 and standard deviation 2.2. Assuming that the new scores are also normally distributed with standard deviation 2.2, investigate whether the mean score for the new ice cream was lower than that of the existing one. Use a 5% significance level.

4 The mean diastolic blood pressure for females is 77.4 mm. A random sample of 118 female computer operators each had their diastolic blood pressure measured. The mean diastolic blood pressure for this sample was 78.8 mm with a standard deviation of 7.1 mm. Investigate, at the 5% significance level, whether there is any evidence to suggest that female computer operators have a mean diastolic blood pressure higher than 77.4 mm.

5 Batteries supplied to a large institution for use in electric clocks had a mean working life of 960 days with a standard deviation of 135 days.

A sample from a new supplier had working lives of

1040   998   894   968   890
1280   1302   798   894   1350 days.

Assume that the data may be regarded as a random sample from a normal distribution.

Investigate whether the batteries from the new supplier have a longer working life than those from the original one. Use a 5% significance level and assume that the standard deviation of the batteries from the new supplier is also 135 days.

6 A chamber of commerce claims that the average take-home pay of manual workers in full-time employment in its area is £140 per week. A sample of 125 such workers had mean take-home pay of £148 and standard deviation £28.

   (a) Test, at the 5% significance level, the hypothesis that the mean take-home pay of all manual workers in the area is £140. Assume that the sample is random and that the distribution of take-home pay is normal. State clearly your null and alternative hypotheses.

   (b) How would your conclusion be affected if you later discovered that:

   (i) the distribution of take-home pay was not normal but the sample was random,

   (ii) the sample was not random but the distribution of take-home pay was normal?

   Give a brief justification for each of your answers.   [A]

7 A pharmaceutical company claimed that a course of its vitamin tablets would improve examination performance. To publicise its claim, the company offered to provide the tablets free to candidates taking a particular GCSE examination. This offer was taken up by some but not all of the candidates. The average mark in the examination for all candidates who did not take the course of vitamin tablets was 42.0.

A random sample of 120 candidates from those who had taken the course of vitamin tablets gave a mean mark of 43.8 and a standard deviation of 12.8.

   (a) Test, at the 5% significance level, whether the candidates who took the vitamin tablets had a mean mark greater than 42.0. State clearly your null and alternative hypotheses.

   (b) Why was it not necessary to know that the examination marks were normally distributed before carrying out the test?

   (c) Explain why, even if the mean mark of the sample had been much higher, the test could not prove that the course of vitamin tablets had improved examination performance.   [A]

Key point summary

1 A hypothesis test needs two hypotheses identified at   *p124*
the beginning: H_0 the **Null Hypothesis** and H_1 the
Alternative Hypothesis.

H_0 and H_1 both refer to the population from which
the sample is randomly taken.

2 H_0 states that a situation is unchanged, that a   *p124*
population parameter takes its usual value.

H_1 states that the parameter has increased, decreased
or just changed.

H_0 states what is to be assumed true unless
overwhelming evidence proves otherwise. In the case
of testing a mean, H_0 is $\mu = k$ for some suggested
value of k.

3 A **two-tailed** test is one where H_1 involves testing   *p125*
for any (non-directional) change in a parameter.

A **one-tailed** test is one where H_1 involves testing
specifically for an increase or for a decrease
(change in one direction only).

A **two-tailed test** results in a critical region with
two areas.

A **one-tailed test** results in a critical region with
one area.

4 The **critical region** or **critical value** identifies the   *p127*
range of extreme values which lead to the **rejection**
of H_0.

The **critical value** is often found directly from
statistical tables as in the case of testing a mean
from a normally distributed population.

5 The **significance level**, α, of a test is the probability   *p127*
that a test statistic lies in the extreme critical region,
if H_0 is true. It determines the level of overwhelming
evidence deemed necessary for the rejection of H_0.

The **significance level**, α, is commonly, but not
exclusively, set at 1%, 5% or 10%.

6 The general procedure for hypothesis testing is: *p127*
  1 Write down H_0 and H_1
  2 Decide which test to use
  3 Decide on the significance level
  4 Identify the critical region
  5 Calculate the test statistic
  6 Draw your conclusion.

7 The **test statistic** used for investigating a hypothesis *p125* regarding the mean of a normally distributed population is,

$$\frac{\bar{x} - \mu}{\frac{\sigma}{\sqrt{n}}}$$

Where $\bar{x}$ is the mean of the randomly selected sample of size n and σ is the known population standard deviation.

If the **test statistic** lies **in** the **critical region**, or beyond the **critical value, H_0** is rejected.

8 Errors which can occur are: *p134*

A **Type 1** error which is to reject **H_0** when it is true.

A **Type 2** error which is to accept **H_0** when it is not true.

The probability of making a **Type 1** error is usually denoted by α.

9 To carry out a hypothesis test for a mean based on   *p138* a **large** sample from an **unspecified** distribution:

the **test statistic** is $\dfrac{\bar{x} - \mu}{\frac{\sigma}{\sqrt{n}}}$.

An estimate of the standard deviation, σ, can be made from the sample, the **test statistic** is compared to **critical z-values**. These are found in AQA Table 4, in the Appendix.

7

Test yourself   What to review

1 Which of the following hypotheses would require a one-tailed   *Section 7.2* test and which a two-tailed test?

  (a) Amphetamines stimulate motor performance. The mean reaction time for those subjects who have taken amphetamine tablets will be slower than that for those who have not.

  (b) The mean score on a new aptitude test for a precision job is claimed to be lower than the mean of 43 found on the existing test.

  (c) Patients suffering from asthma have a higher mean health conscious index than people who do not suffer from asthma.

  (d) The mean length of rods has changed since the overhaul of a machine.

2 What is the name given to the value with which a test statistic   *Section 7.4* is compared in order to decide whether a null hypothesis should be rejected?

Test yourself (*continued*)	What to review

3 (a) What is the name given to the agreed probability of wrongly rejecting a null hypothesis?

(b) Give three commonly used levels for this probability.

Section 7.4

---

4 A manufacturer collects data on the annual maintenance costs for a random selection of eight new welding machines.

The mean cost of these eight machines is found to be £54.36. The standard deviation of such costs for welding machines is £8.74.

Stating the null and alternative hypotheses, and using a 1% significance level, test whether there is any evidence that the mean cost for maintenance of the new machines is less than the mean value of £71.90 found for the old welding machines.

Section 7.5

---

5 In a survey of workers who travel to work at a large factory by car, the distances, in km, travelled by a random sample of ten workers were:

14   43   17   52   22   25   68   32   26   44

In previous surveys, the mean distance was found to be 35.6 km with a standard deviation of 14.5 km.

(a) Investigate, using a 5% significance level, whether the mean distance travelled to work has changed. Assume the standard deviation remains 14.5 km.

(b) What is the meaning of:

(i) a **Type 1** error,

(ii) a **Type 2** error,

in the context of this question?

(c) Why is it important that the sample of workers is selected at random from all those factory workers who travel to work by car?

Sections 7.3, 7.5 and 7.7

---

6 What is the rule which is commonly used to determine whether a sample is **large**?

Section 7.8

Test yourself **ANSWERS**

6 n at least 30.

5 (a) ts -0.284 cv ± 1.96 no change;

(b) (i) conclude there has been a change when in fact there has not,

(ii) conclude no change when in fact there has been a change;

(c) Conclusion unreliable if sample not random. For example, sample may have been taken only from white collar workers who may have a different mean travelling distance from manual workers.

4 ts -5.68 cv -2.3263 mean cost is less.

3 (a) Significance level;   **(b)** 1%, 5%, 10%.

2 Critical value.

1 (a) one-tail;   **(b)** one-tail;   **(c)** one-tail;   **(d)** two-tail.

Exam style practice paper

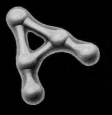

Time allowed 1 hour 45 minutes

Answer **all** questions

1 The owner of a number of national newspapers bids to buy a famous football club. A large number of the club's supporters write letters to the editors of these newspapers. Of these letters 90% are against the bid, 4% are neutral and 6% are in favour of the bid.

(a) If two letters are selected at random find the probability that:

(i) they will both be against the bid, *(2 marks)*

(ii) one will be against the bid and one will be neutral. *(2 marks)*

(b) If three letters are chosen at random find the probability that two or more will be against the bid. *(3 marks)*

The probability of a letter being published is:

0.01 if it is against the bid

0.24 if it is neutral

0.65 if it is in favour of the bid.

(c) Find the probability that a randomly selected letter is:

(i) against the bid and is published, *(2 marks)*

(ii) published. *(3 marks)*

2 The lengths of cod caught by a fishing boat may be regarded as a random sample from a normal distribution with mean 74 cm and standard deviation 10 cm.

(a) Find the probability that:

   (i) the length of a randomly selected cod is between 70 cm and 75 cm, *(5 marks)*

   (ii) the mean length of 90 randomly selected cod is more than 73 cm. *(3 marks)*

(b) What length is exceeded by the longest 10% of the cod. *(3 marks)*

(c) Would your answer to part **(a) (ii)** still be valid if it was discovered that:

   (i) the sample was not random but the distribution was normal,

   (ii) the distribution was not normal but the sample was random?

   Explain your answers. *(4 marks)*

3 Applicants for an assembly job take a test of manual dexterity. Current employees took an average of 60 s to complete the test. The times, in seconds, taken to complete the test by a random sample of applicants were,

   63   125   77   49   74   67   59   66   102

(a) Stating clearly your null and alternative hypotheses, investigate, at the 5% significance level, whether the mean time taken by applicants to complete the test is greater than that taken by current employees. Assume that the standard deviation of the times is 19 s. *(7 marks)*

(b) It later emerged that due to a misunderstanding of how the test should be timed all the recorded times for the new applicants were five seconds too long. Does this further information affect your conclusion in **(a)**? *(4 marks)*

4 The table below shows, for each of a sample of countries, the population, in millions, and the number of medals won at the 1992 Summer Olympic Games plus those won at the 1994 Winter Olympic Games. The final column shows the number of these medals which were won at the 1994 Winter Olympic Games.

Country	Population, x	Total number of medals won at 1992 Summer and 1994 Winter games, y	Number of medals won at 1994 Winter games, z
Britain	58	22	2
Canada	28	31	13
Cuba	11	31	0
Italy	58	39	20
Jamaica	3	4	0
North Korea	23	15	6
Poland	39	19	0
Sweden	9	15	3
Unified Team	232	146	34
United States	261	122	13

(a) Draw a scatter diagram of the population, x, and the total number of medals won, y. *(2 marks)*

(b) Calculate the equation of the regression line of total number of medals won on population. Draw this line on your scatter diagram. *(6 marks)*

The Unified Team was made up of athletes from countries, including Russia, which were formerly part of the USSR.

(c) Use your regression equation to predict how many medals would have been won by Russia (population 150 million) if it had competed separately from the other countries in the Unified Team. *(1 mark)*

(d) State, giving a reason, whether you think the prediction made in **(c)** is likely to be an underestimate or an overestimate. *(2 marks)*

(e) Calculate the product moment correlation coefficient between the number of medals won at the 1992 Summer Olympic Games and the number of medals won at the 1994 Winter Olympic Games. *(4 marks)*

(f) Interpret the correlation coefficient you have calculated in **(e)** in the context of this data. *(2 marks)*

(g) Identify two features of the data which suggest that the sample is not a random sample of all countries. *(2 marks)*

5 A 'safer routes to school' campaign is to be undertaken by a city council which wishes to encourage parents and children to walk or cycle to school rather than to use private cars. As a first step it is decided to estimate the mean distance travelled to school by junior school children. In a pilot study the following distances, in miles, travelled by a sample of children in the city were obtained:

1.2   0.1   0.7   0.8   0.2   0.1   3.9   0.3   0.1   1.1

(a) Calculate a 95% confidence interval for the mean distance travelled to school by all junior school children in the city. Take the standard deviation to be 0.90 miles. *(8 marks)*

(b) State two assumptions (apart from the value of the standard deviation) you needed to make in order to answer (a). *(2 marks)*

(c) Does the data provide any reason to suspect that one necessary assumption may not be true? Explain your answer. *(2 marks)*

In a larger survey, a random sample of 140 junior school children in the city were found to travel a mean distance of 1.01 miles with a standard deviation of 0.98 miles.

(d) Calculate a 90% confidence interval for the mean distance travelled to school by junior school children in the city. *(4 marks)*

(e) Explain why you did not need to make any assumptions to calculate the confidence interval in (d). *(2 marks)*

(f) Find, approximately, the size of sample necessary to obtain an 80% confidence interval of width 0.1 miles for the mean distance travelled by junior school children in the city. *(5 marks)*

Appendix

Table 3 Normal distribution function

The table gives the probability p that a normally distributed random variable Z, with mean = 0 and variance = 1, is less than or equal to z.

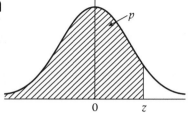

z	0.00	0.01	0.02	0.03	0.04	0.05	0.06	0.07	0.08	0.09	z
0.0	0.50000	0.50399	0.50798	0.51197	0.51595	0.51994	0.52392	0.52790	0.53188	0.53586	0.0
0.1	0.53983	0.54380	0.54776	0.55172	0.55567	0.55962	0.56356	0.56749	0.57142	0.57535	0.1
0.2	0.57926	0.58317	0.58706	0.59095	0.59483	0.59871	0.60257	0.60642	0.61026	0.61409	0.2
0.3	0.61791	0.62172	0.62552	0.62930	0.63307	0.63683	0.64058	0.64431	0.64803	0.65173	0.3
0.4	0.65542	0.65910	0.66276	0.66640	0.67003	0.67364	0.67724	0.68082	0.68439	0.68793	0.4
0.5	0.69146	0.69497	0.69847	0.70194	0.70540	0.70884	0.71226	0.71566	0.71904	0.72240	0.5
0.6	0.72575	0.72907	0.73237	0.73565	0.73891	0.74215	0.74537	0.74857	0.75175	0.75490	0.6
0.7	0.75804	0.76115	0.76424	0.76730	0.77035	0.77337	0.77637	0.77935	0.78230	0.78524	0.7
0.8	0.78814	0.79103	0.79389	0.79673	0.79955	0.80234	0.80511	0.80785	0.81057	0.81327	0.8
0.9	0.81594	0.81859	0.82121	0.82381	0.82639	0.82894	0.83147	0.83398	0.83646	0.83891	0.9
1.0	0.84134	0.84375	0.84614	0.84849	0.85083	0.85314	0.85543	0.85769	0.85993	0.86214	1.0
1.1	0.86433	0.86650	0.86864	0.87076	0.87286	0.87493	0.87698	0.87900	0.88100	0.88298	1.1
1.2	0.88493	0.88686	0.88877	0.89065	0.89251	0.89435	0.89617	0.89796	0.89973	0.90147	1.2
1.3	0.90320	0.90490	0.90658	0.90824	0.90988	0.91149	0.91309	0.91466	0.91621	0.91774	1.3
1.4	0.91924	0.92073	0.92220	0.92364	0.92507	0.92647	0.92785	0.92922	0.93056	0.93189	1.4
1.5	0.93319	0.93448	0.93574	0.93699	0.93822	0.93943	0.94062	0.94179	0.94295	0.94408	1.5
1.6	0.94520	0.94630	0.94738	0.94845	0.94950	0.95053	0.95154	0.95254	0.95352	0.95449	1.6
1.7	0.95543	0.95637	0.95728	0.95818	0.95907	0.95994	0.96080	0.96164	0.96246	0.96327	1.7
1.8	0.96407	0.96485	0.96562	0.96638	0.96712	0.96784	0.96856	0.96926	0.96995	0.97062	1.8
1.9	0.97128	0.97193	0.97257	0.97320	0.97381	0.97441	0.97500	0.97558	0.97615	0.97670	1.9
2.0	0.97725	0.97778	0.97831	0.97882	0.97932	0.97982	0.98030	0.98077	0.98124	0.98169	2.0
2.1	0.98214	0.98257	0.98300	0.98341	0.98382	0.98422	0.98461	0.98500	0.98537	0.98574	2.1
2.2	0.98610	0.98645	0.98679	0.98679	0.98713	0.98745	0.98778	0.98809	0.98840	0.98899	2.2
2.3	0.98928	0.98956	0.98983	0.99010	0.99036	0.99061	0.99086	0.99111	0.99134	0.99158	2.3
2.4	0.99180	0.99202	0.99224	0.99245	0.99266	0.99286	0.99305	0.99324	0.99343	0.99361	2.4
2.5	0.99379	0.99396	0.99413	0.99430	0.99446	0.99461	0.99477	0.99492	0.99506	0.99520	2.5
2.6	0.99534	0.99547	0.99560	0.99573	0.99585	0.99598	0.99609	0.99621	0.99632	0.99643	2.6
2.7	0.99653	0.99664	0.99674	0.99683	0.99693	0.99702	0.99711	0.99720	0.99728	0.99736	2.7
2.8	0.99744	0.99752	0.99760	0.99767	0.99774	0.99781	0.99788	0.99795	0.99801	0.99807	2.8
2.9	0.99813	0.99819	0.99825	0.99831	0.99836	0.99841	0.99846	0.99851	0.99856	0.99861	2.9
3.0	0.99865	0.99869	0.99874	0.99878	0.99882	0.99886	0.99889	0.99893	0.99896	0.99900	3.0
3.1	0.99903	0.99906	0.99910	0.99913	0.99916	0.99918	0.99921	0.99924	0.99926	0.99929	3.1
3.2	0.99931	0.99934	0.99936	0.99938	0.99940	0.99942	0.99944	0.99946	0.99948	0.99950	3.2
3.3	0.99952	0.99953	0.99955	0.99957	0.99958	0.99960	0.99961	0.99962	0.99964	0.99965	3.3
3.4	0.99966	0.99968	0.99969	0.99970	0.99971	0.99972	0.99973	0.99974	0.99975	0.99976	3.4
3.5	0.99977	0.99978	0.99978	0.99979	0.99980	0.99981	0.99981	0.99982	0.99983	0.99983	3.5
3.6	0.99984	0.99985	0.99985	0.99986	0.99986	0.99987	0.99987	0.99988	0.99988	0.99989	3.6
3.7	0.99989	0.99990	0.99990	0.99990	0.99991	0.99991	0.99992	0.99992	0.99992	0.99992	3.7
3.8	0.99993	0.99993	0.99993	0.99994	0.99994	0.99994	0.99994	0.99995	0.99995	0.99995	3.8
3.9	0.99995	0.99995	0.99996	0.99996	0.99996	0.99996	0.99996	0.99996	0.99997	0.99997	3.9

Table 4 Percentage points of the normal distribution

The table gives the values of z satisfying $P(Z \leq z) = p$,
where Z is the normally distributed random variable
with mean = 0 and variance = 1.

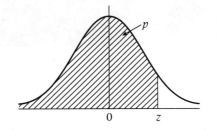

p	0.00	0.01	0.02	0.03	0.04	0.05	0.06	0.07	0.08	0.09	p
0.5	0.0000	0.0251	0.0502	0.0753	0.1004	0.1257	0.1510	0.1764	0.2019	0.2275	0.5
0.6	0.2533	0.2793	0.3055	0.3319	0.3585	0.3853	0.4125	0.4399	0.4677	0.4958	0.6
0.7	0.5244	0.5534	0.5828	0.6128	0.6433	0.6745	0.7063	0.7388	0.7722	0.8064	0.7
0.8	0.8416	0.8779	0.9154	0.9542	0.9945	1.0364	1.0803	1.1264	1.1750	1.2265	0.8
0.9	1.2816	1.3408	1.4051	1.4758	1.5548	1.6449	1.7507	1.8808	2.0537	2.3263	0.9

p	0.000	0.001	0.002	0.003	0.004	0.005	0.006	0.007	0.008	0.009	p
0.95	1.6449	1.6546	1.6646	1.6747	1.6849	1.6954	1.7060	1.7169	1.7279	1.7392	0.95
0.96	1.7507	1.7624	1.7744	1.7866	1.7991	1.8119	1.8250	1.8384	1.8522	1.8663	0.96
0.97	1.8808	1.8957	1.9110	1.9268	1.9431	1.9600	1.9774	1.9954	2.0141	2.0335	0.97
0.98	2.0537	2.0749	2.0969	2.1201	2.1444	2.1701	2.1973	2.2262	2.2571	2.2904	0.98
0.99	2.3263	2.3656	2.4089	2.4573	2.5121	2.5758	2.6521	2.7478	2.8782	3.0902	0.99

Answers

1 Collection of data

EXERCISE 1A

1 **(a)** Qualitative;

   (b) Discrete quantitative;

   (c) Continuous quantitative (but age in years is discrete);

   (d) Continuous quantitative;

   (e) Qualitative;

   (f) Discrete quantitative;

   (g) Discrete quantitative;

   (h) Continuous quantitative;

   (i) Discrete quantitative;

   (j) Qualitative.

EXERCISE 1B

1 In this question more than one answer is possible. You may find answers in addition to those given below.

   (a) The populations mentioned in the passage will relate to all first division matches in 1999/2000 and are either the results, the total number of goals scored or the amounts of time played before a goal is scored;

   (b) The total numbers of goals scored in each match played on the first Saturday of the season;

   (c) Mean number of goals per match for the 1999/2000 season;

   (d) Mean number of goals per match on the first Saturday of the season;

   (e) The result of matches (home, away or draw);

   (f) Number of goals scored in each match (the mean number of goals scored in each match is also discrete. For example if 100 matches were played the only possible outcomes are 0.00, 0.01, 0.02 ..., however, the steps will be so small that this could also be treated as a continuous variable);

   (g) The amounts of time played before a goal is scored;

   (h) The data the journalist collected in the 1999/2000 season;

   (i) The mean number of goals per game in the previous season.

2 (a) Place of birth, sex;

(b) Height, weight;

(c) Number of pupils weighed (age in years and months is also discrete although exact age is continuous);

(d) The data collected at the medical examination;

(e) The data collected by the class;

(f) The weights of all second year pupils;

(g) The weights of those second year pupils who were weighed;

(h) Mean weight of a sample of pupils.

EXERCISE 1C

1 Number books 0000 to 2124. Select four-digit random numbers. Ignore repeats and >2124. Continue until 20 numbers obtained. Select corresponding books.

2 Obtain list of employees names and number 000 to 711. Select three-digit random numbers. Ignore repeats and >711. Continue until six numbers obtained. Select corresponding employees.

3 Number the plants 00 to 27. Select two-digit random numbers. Ignore repeats and >27. Continue until eight numbers obtained. Select corresponding plants.

4 (a) There are 36 students ages. Allocate the number 00 to the first age (19), the number 01 to the second age (20) ... allocate the number 35 to the last age (27).

Select two digit random numbers ignoring >35

62 50 62 27 80 30 72 07 93 38 68 35 86 27 65 33
        27   38   19   27   27   41

The ages selected are 27, 38, 19, 27, 27, 41 (answers will vary according to your starting point in the random number tables);

(b) As in **(a)** except that now repeats of random numbers are ignored.

62 50 62 27 80 30 72 07 93 38 68 35 86 27 65 33 40 18
        27   38   19   27   41   20

The ages selected are 27, 38, 19, 27, 41, 20.

5 Number rods 000 to 499. Select three-digit random numbers. Ignore repeats and >499. Continue until 20 numbers selected. Choose corresponding rods.

6 (a) No, because not all sets of 40 customers can be chosen;

(b) Number names 0000 to 8949. Select four-digit random numbers. Ignore repeats and >8949. Continue until 40 numbers selected. Choose corresponding names.

7 No, because not all sets of 128 electors can be selected.

2 Probability

EXERCISE 2A

1 (a) 0.05;   (b) 0.25;   (c) 0.3;   (d) 0.1.

2 (a) $\dfrac{1}{7}$;   (b) $\dfrac{2}{7}$;   (c) $\dfrac{4}{7}$.

3 (a) $\dfrac{1}{7}$;   (b) $\dfrac{4}{7}$;   (c) $\dfrac{5}{7}$.

4 (a) $\dfrac{7}{15}$;   (b) $\dfrac{1}{3}$;   (c) $\dfrac{4}{5}$;   (d) 0;   (e) $\dfrac{1}{3}$.

5 (a) $\dfrac{1}{11}$;   (b) $\dfrac{3}{11}$;   (c) $\dfrac{9}{11}$;   (d) $\dfrac{3}{11}$.

EXERCISE 2B

1 0.4.

2 0.78.

3 (a) 0.6;   (b) 0.5;   (c) 0.9.

4 (a) 0.7;   (b) 0.4;   (c) 0.8;   (d) 0.7;   (e) 0.2.

5 (a) $\dfrac{27}{35}$;   (b) $\dfrac{32}{35}$;   (c) $\dfrac{3}{35}$;   (d) $\dfrac{23}{35}$.

6 (a) (i) A, B,   (ii) A, C or B, C;

   (b) the event that the baby will not have blue eyes.

7 (a) A;   (b) yes;   (c) B, C.

EXERCISE 2C

1 0.42.

2 0.022.

3 0.25.

4 (a) 0.01;   (b) 0.81.

5 0.125.

EXERCISE 2D

Answers to three significant figures.

1 (a) 0.165;   (b) 0.48;   (c) 0.615.

2 (a) (i) 0.846,   (ii) 0.147,   (iii) 0.154;

   (b) (i) 0.779,   (ii) 0.203,   (iii) 0.0182.

3 (a) (i) 0.0625, **(ii)** 0.375;

   (b) (i) 0.422, **(ii)** 0.141, **(iii)** 0.156, **(iv)** 0.844;

   (c) 0.316.

4 (a) (i) 0.64, **(ii)** 0.24, **(iii)** 0.665,

       (iv) 0.9025, **(v)** 0.335;

   (b) (i) 0.512, **(ii)** 0.288, **(iii)** 0.008,

       (iv) 0.5155, **(v)** 0.036.

EXERCISE 2E

1 (a) $\frac{5}{8}$; **(b)** $\frac{2}{3}$; **(c)** $\frac{3}{8}$; **(d)** $\frac{47}{120}$; **(e)** $\frac{9}{10}$;

  (f) $\frac{47}{80}$; **(g)** $\frac{28}{75}$; **(h)** $\frac{7}{10}$; **(i)** $\frac{33}{80}$; **(j)** $\frac{7}{30}$.

2 (a) $\frac{23}{30}$; **(b)** $\frac{121}{150}$; **(c)** $\frac{25}{29}$; **(d)** $\frac{119}{150}$; **(e)** $\frac{1}{6}$;

  (f) $\frac{3}{5}$; **(g)** $\frac{2}{5}$; **(h)** $\frac{90}{121}$; **(i)** $\frac{31}{35}$.

3 (a) $\frac{4}{9}$; **(b)** $\frac{2}{3}$; **(c)** $\frac{5}{9}$; **(d)** $\frac{2}{15}$; **(e)** $\frac{4}{5}$;

  (f) $\frac{13}{23}$; **(g)** $\frac{1}{5}$; **(h)** $\frac{7}{10}$; **(i)** 0.

A and C not independent.

EXERCISE 2F

Answers to three significant figures.

1 (a) 0.195; **(b)** 0.499.

2 (a) 0.357; **(b)** 0.536.

3 (a) (i) 0.0152, **(ii)** 0.182, **(iii)** 0.227;

   (b) (i) 0.0909, **(ii)** 0.136, **(iii)** 0.409, **(iv)** 0.218.

4 (a) 0.0480; **(b)** 0.506; **(c)** 0.305.

5 (a) 0.196; **(b)** 0.0240; **(c)** 0.0840; **(d)** 0.0960;

  (e) 0.240; **(f)** 0.228; **(g)** 0.192.

6 (a) 0.0461; **(b)** 0.233; **(c)** 0.0121; **(d)** 0.279;

  (e) 0.0101; **(f)** 0.266; **(g)** 0.152.

MIXED EXERCISE

1 (a) $\frac{1}{343}$; **(b)** $\frac{1}{49}$; **(c)** $\frac{30}{49}$; **(d)** $\frac{8}{343}$; **(e)** 6.

2 (a) (i) 0.576, **(ii)** 0.932; **(b)** 0.912.

3 (a) 0.0429; **(b)** 0.142; **(c)** 0.1215;
(d) 0.189; **(e)** 0.334.

4 (a) (i) 0.36, **(ii)** 0.09, **(iii)** 0.89, **(iv)** 0.36;
(b) $(R'$ and $T')$ [or $(R$ or $T)'$].

5 (a) (i) 0.343, **(ii)** 0.441;
(b) (i) 0.063, **(ii)** 0.09; **(c)** 0.141.

6 (a) (i) 0.12, **(ii)** 0.0455, **(iii)** 0.318,
(iv) 0.0133, **(v)** 0.893;
(b) 0.0827.

7 (a) (i) 0.462, **(ii)** 0.223, **(iii)** 0.808, **(iv)** 0.517;
(b) (i) 0.1575, **(ii)** 0.153; **(c)** 0.224.

3 The normal distribution

EXERCISE 3A

1 (a) 0.891; **(b)** 0.834; **(c)** 0.968;
(d) 0.663; **(e)** 0.536; **(f)** 0.942;
(g) 0.974; **(h)** 0.726; **(i)** 0.991;
(j) 0.853.

EXERCISE 3B

1 (a) 0.0869; **(b)** 0.281; **(c)** 0.109;
(d) 0.195; **(e)** 0.374; **(f)** 0.0262;
(g) 0.00889; **(h)** 0.258; **(i)** 0.464;
(j) 0.0885.

EXERCISE 3C

1 (a) 0.823; **(b)** 0.281; **(c)** 0.862;
(d) 0.681; **(e)** 0.326; **(f)** 0.626;
(g) 0.261; **(h)** 0.802; **(i)** 0.773;
(j) 0.330.

EXERCISE 3D

1 (a) 0.209; **(b)** 0.0948; **(c)** 0.516;
(d) 0.877; **(e)** 0.112; **(f)** 0.0214;
(g) 0.888; **(h)** 0.003 61; **(i)** 0.0792;
(j) 0.968.

EXERCISE 3E

1 (a) 1.4; (b) 0.6; (c) −0.8;
   (d) −1.6; (e) 2.1.

2 (a) 0.652; (b) −1.370;
   (c) 1.348; (d) −1.804.

3 (a) 1.167; (b) −0.167;
   (c) 0.667; (d) −1.167.

EXERCISE 3F

1 (a) 0.663; (b) 0.104; (c) 0.134;
   (d) 0.943; (e) 0.396; (f) 0.256.

2 (a) 0.779; (b) 0.663; (c) 0.0336;
   (d) 0.0367; (e) 0.913; (f) 0.295.

3 (a) 0.245; (b) 0.755; (c) 0.832;
   (d) 0.152; (e) 0.659; (f) 0.603.

4 (a) 0.637; (b) 0.0838; (c) 0.0455;
   (d) 0.705; (e) 0.179; (f) 0.395.

5 (a) 0.230; (b) 0.152; (c) 0.858.

EXERCISE 3G

1 (a) +1.960; (b) −1.282; (c) −1.645;
   (d) +1.44 (using interpolation); (e) −1.960;
   (f) +1.036; (g) −0.842; (h) +1.282;
   (i) +2.326.

2 (a) −1.645 and +1.645;
   (b) −2.576 and +2.576;
   (c) −3.090 and +3.090.

EXERCISE 3H

1 (a) 85.5; (b) 80.1; (c) 69.3;
   (d) 88.8; (e) 59.2–88.8; (f) 66.4–81.6.

2 (a) 421; (b) 370; (c) 355;
   (d) 321; (e) 231; (f) 277–433.

3 (a) 2.35 (35 minutes past 2 – answer to nearest minute to ensure
        arriving **before** 3.00);
   (b) 2.30; (c) 2.26; (d) 2.46;
   (e) 2.40 (nearest minute to arrive **after** 3.00);
   (f) 2.47.

EXERCISE 3I

1 26.78–31.62 cm.

2 (a) (i) 0.894, **(ii)** 0.493;

(b) Longest possible stay is 60 minutes. For proposed model about 60% of times will exceed 60 minutes. Model could not apply;

(c) 99.9% of normal distribution less than $\mu + 3\sigma$, i.e. $65 + 3 \times 20 = 125$ minutes. Model could be plausible for users entering 125 minutes or more before closing time, i.e. 6.55 p.m.

Note: this answer is very cautious, you could argue that 95% of the distribution is sufficient.

3 (a) 0.405; **(b)** £761; **(c)** 0.0269;

(d) Cannot be exact because money is a discrete variable and also because negative takings impossible.

EXERCISE 3J

Interpolation has been used, your answers may be slightly different if you have not used interpolation.

1 (a) 0.909; **(b)** 0.0710; **(c)** 0.838.

2 (a) 45.75 – 46.65 cm;

(b) 46.58 cm;

(c) 128.

3 (a) (i) 0.122, **(ii)** 0.661, **(iii)** 0.488;

(b) 15.6 – 20.4 s.

4 (a) 129;

(b) Large sample → sample mean normally distributed, whatever the population distribution;

(c) Might be invalid if sample size small and population not normal (or sample not random).

MIXED EXERCISE

1 (a) 0.291 or 29.1%; **(b)** 403.

2 0.841.

3 (a) 0.159; **(b)** 0.801; **(c)** 60.2 g.

4 (a) 0.919; **(b)** 0.274; **(c)** 8.11 a.m.

5 (a) 0.022 75; **(b)** 0.821;

(c) 0.0886 (answers may be slightly different without interpolation).

Large sample in **(c)** so answer unchanged if weights not normally distributed.

6 0.0475 or 4.75%. **7** 0.910.

8 (a) 0.401; **(b)** 0.691; **(c)** 0.494, unaffected.

9 (a) 0.212 or 21.2%; **(b)** 22.6 g.

10 (a) 0.386; **(b)** 0.0644.

Money is discrete variable normal is continuous; cannot carry a negative amount of change.

11 (a) 0.115; **(b)** 33.2 g.

12 (a) 0.685; **(b)** 40.5 m;

(c) 40 m, 4.9 m; **(d)** Gwen.

13 (a) (i) 0.0495, **(ii)** 0.000 05,

I and II aren't satisfied.

(b) (i) 105.3 ml, **(ii)** 106.5 ml,

mean at least 106.5 ml;

(c) (i) 103.3 ml (mean), 3.98 ml (sd),

(ii) Yes, conditions just met, but if sd reduced, conditions can be met with smaller mean content.

4 Correlation

EXERCISE 4A

1 (a) (i) yes, **(ii)** yes, **(iii)** no;

(b) (i) No – all points do not lie on the same line,

(ii) Yes – weak, negative correlation is evident,

(iii) No – $-1 \le r \le 1$ so $r = 1.2$ is impossible.

2 (a) 0.9; **(b)** −0.3; **(c)** 0.85; **(d)** 0.

3 (a) and **(b) (i)**

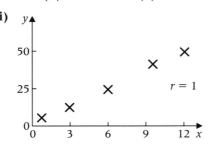

(ii)

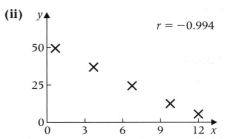

(iii)

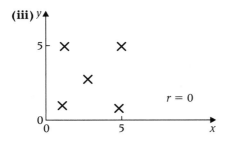

(iv)

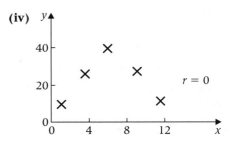

4 **(b)** $\bar{x} = 56.9$, $\bar{y} = 27.7$;

  (c) $S_{xx} = 16\,570.9$, $S_{yy} = 3568.9$

  $r = 0.880$.

  (a) and **(b)**

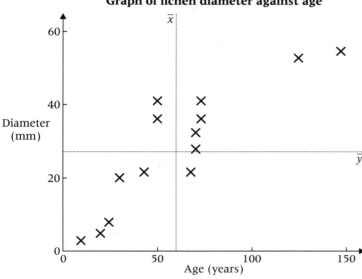

Graph of lichen diameter against age

5 (a) and **(c)**

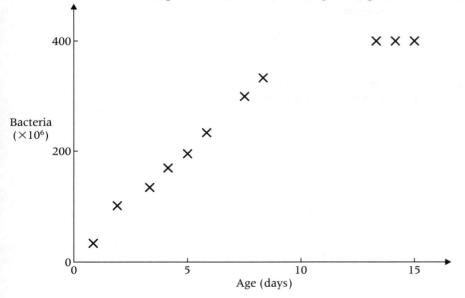

Graph of number of bacteria against age

  (b) $r = 0.989$;

  (c) Although a very strong correlation was found in **(b)**, it appears
    that the rate of growth is decreasing, i.e. the linear relationship
    will probably not continue.

6

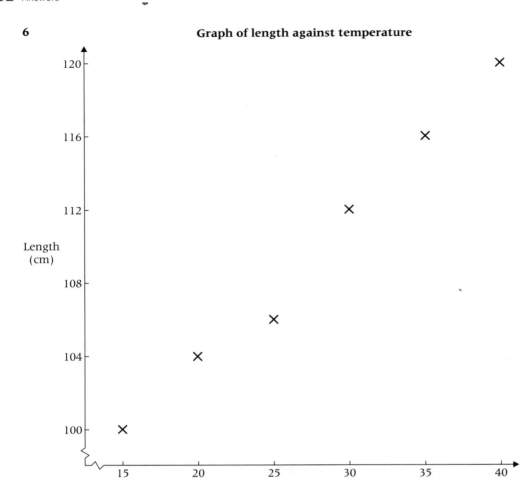

Graph of length against temperature

$r = 0.995$.

Discard $(25, 106.1) \rightarrow$ new $r = 0.99991$, $r \approx 1$.

It appears there is an exact linear relationship once $(25, 106.1)$ is removed. However, even when including this point the fit was very good.

7 (a)

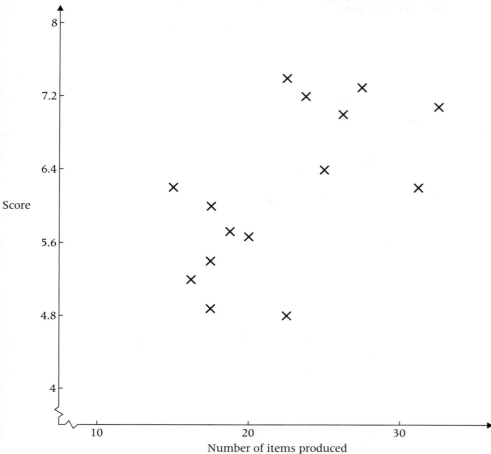

Graph of score against number produced

(b) $r = 0.610$;

(c) The data appear to show that the owner's belief is incorrect as there is weak positive correlation. However, if the data were divided into two groups, the owner's belief may be true as the experienced craftsmen (2, 4, 8, 9, 10, 13, 14 perhaps) may produce higher quality goods, but this quality may deteriorate if rushed.

8 (a)

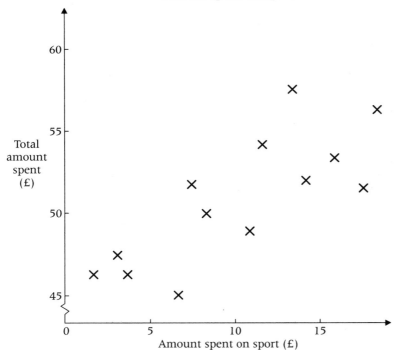

Graph of total amount spent against amount spent on sport

(b) $r = 0.824$;

(c) It appears appropriate since the data seem to follow a linear relationship. Since x is part of y, it might be better to examine relationship of x with $y - x$.

9 (b) $r = 0.937$;

(c) Calculations seem inappropriate as a clear non-linear relationship is seen – despite high value of r.

10 (a) $r = -0.800$;

(b) $r = -0.817$;

(c) Both values for r show fairly strong negative correlation indicating **(a)** higher heart value function links to lower baldness and **(b)** higher hours of TV links to lower heart function;

(d) Data does not provide evidence for a causal link between watching TV and any effect on heart function. There may be a separate factor which is linked to both number of hours watching TV and heart function.

5 Regression

EXERCISE 5A

1 (a)

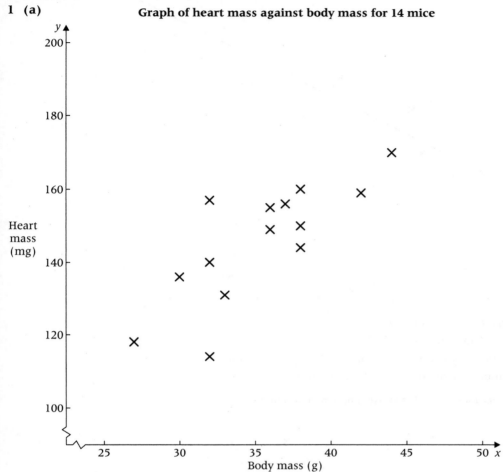

Graph of heart mass against body mass for 14 mice

(b) $y = 48.4 + 2.75x$.

2 (a)

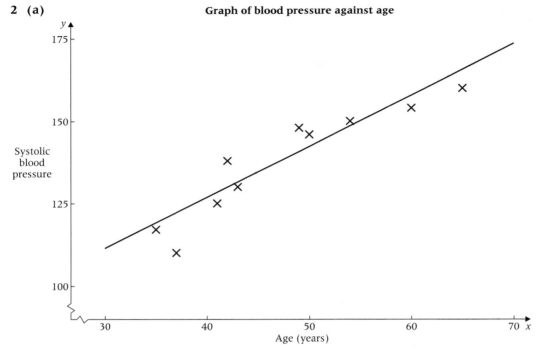

Graph of blood pressure against age

(b) $y = 62.8 + 1.58x$;

(c) **(i)** $y = 1.5763 \times 20 + 62.766 = 94.3$,

    (ii) $y = 1.5763 \times 45 + 62.766 = 133.7$;

(d) **(i)** Extrapolation – not accurate, linear model may not continue,

    (ii) Interpolation – likely to be reasonably accurate.

3 (a)   **Graph of hardness of shell against supplement amount**

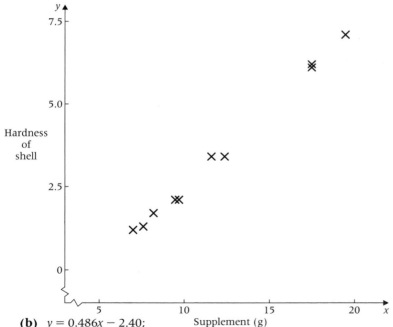

(b) $y = 0.486x - 2.40$;

(c) y on scale 0–10, model cannot extend to values of x outside range 5–25 (approximately).

4 (a) and **(c)**

Graph of predicted age against and actual age

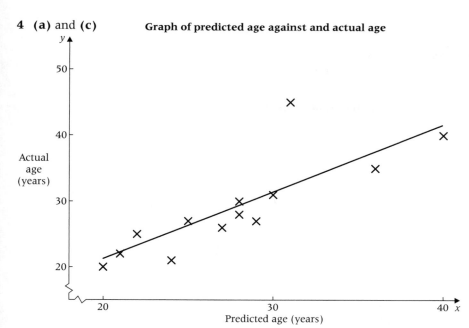

(b) $y = 1.03x + 0.533$;

(d) With the exception of G, predictions seem fairly accurate – the points all lie close to the line. It would be advisable to investigate person G to see if they should be excluded (been ill/in prison?).

5 (a) and **(c)**

Graph of price against capacity

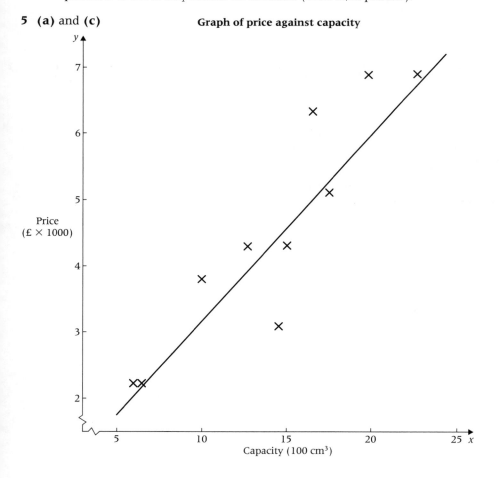

(b) $y = 3.02x + 237$;

(d) Model J is recommended (well below line – very low price).
Discourage models A, E and K (above line – high price).

6 (a)

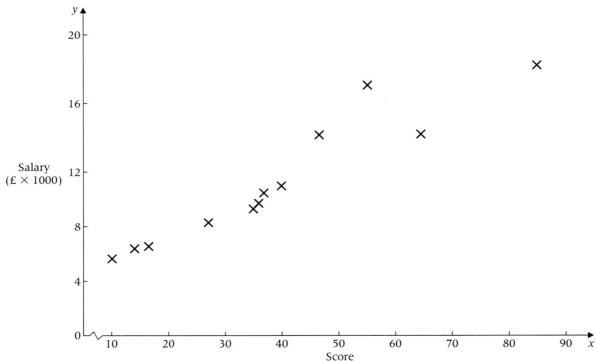

Graph of salary against score

(b) $y = 192x + 3713$;

(c) Points close to straight line, apart from B and C. Method should be
reasonably satisfactory;

(d) Salary $= a + bx + t$, where t is an additional payment for
employees who have to work away from home.

7 (a)

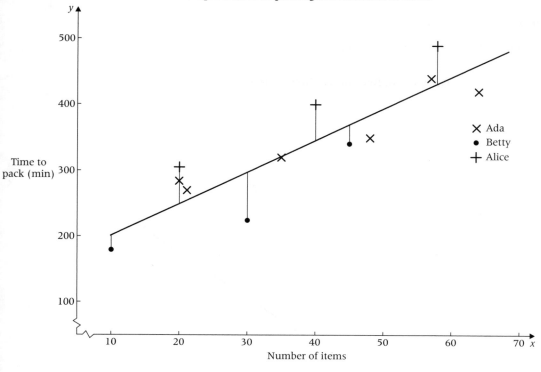

Graph of time to pack against number of items

(b) $r = 0.897$;

(c) $y = 166 + 4.62x$;

(d) $y = 4.6161 \times 45 + 165.52 = 373$, should be fairly accurate but would depend on packer;

(e) Betty $\simeq -59.0, -31.7, -33.2$, average -41.3,
Alice $\simeq +47.2, +49.8, +56.7$, average $+51.2$;

(f) **(i)** Betty $373.2 - 41.3 = 332$,
(ii) Alice $373.2 + 51.2 = 424$.

8 (a)

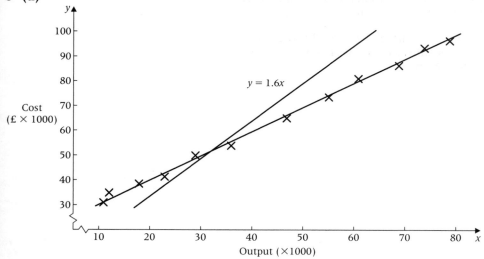

Graph of cost against output

$y = 1.6x$

(b) $y = 0.961x + 20.7$;

(c) Approximately 32 000 output;

(d) If output above 32 000 a quarter, profit will be made.

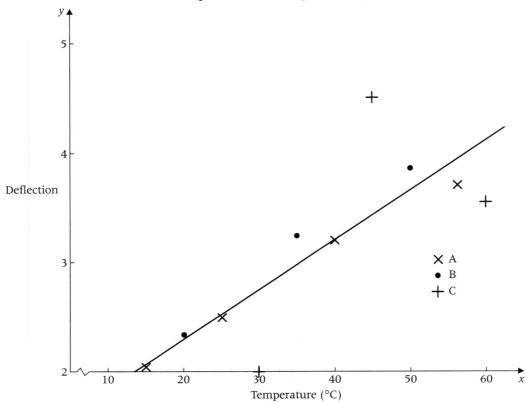

Graph of deflection against temperature

(b) $y = 0.0453x + 1.42$;

(c) Technician *B* seems to give higher results than *A*. *A* and *B* are both consistent, however, *C*'s results are very erratic;

(d) Check which of *A* and *B* is 'accurate'. Try to find and eliminate cause of small systematic difference between *A* and *B*. Check *C*'s measurements: *C* needs retraining.

10 (a)

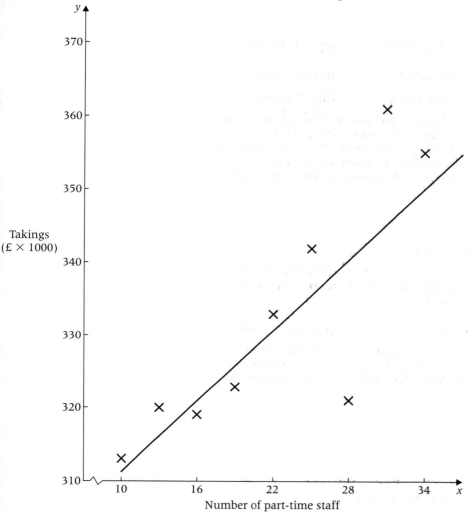

Graph of takings against number of part-time staff

y-axis: Takings (£ × 1000), marked 310, 320, 330, 340, 350, 360, 370

x-axis: Number of part-time staff, marked 10, 16, 22, 28, 34

(b) $y = 294 + 1.73x$;

(c) £29 400, estimate of takings when no part-time staff employed.
£173 extra taken per extra part-time member of staff;

(d) Week with 28 staff – abnormally low takings relative to pattern;

(e) Might be run-up to Christmas and takings would increase
anyway. There may be other outside factors affecting the
experiment. Better to choose random levels of part-time staff.

6 Confidence intervals

EXERCISE 6A

1 **(a)** 58.64–60.00; **(b)** 58.81–59.83; **(c)** 59.10–59.54.

2 **(a)** **(i)** 65.0–82.2, **(ii)** 63.3–83.8, **(iii)** 60.1–87.0;

    (b) **(i)** 83.9–97.3, **(ii)** 80.4–100.8, **(iii)** 77.1–104.1;

    (c) Athletes seem to have a lower mean diastolic blood pressure than for the population of healthy adults (84.8 is above the 95% confidence interval, although it is just inside the 99% interval). On this evidence chess club members are consistent with the population of healthy adults as 84.8 lies within the confidence intervals.

3 63.5–115.5.

4 **(a)** 101.7–159.2; **(b)** 29.3–174.1;

    (c) Station manager's claim is incorrect. Even making the lowest reasonable estimate of the mean the great majority of passengers will queue for more than 25 s.

5 **(a)** 494.69–499.63; **(b)** **(i)** 7.5 g, **(ii)** 440.3–478.9;

    (c) Confidence interval calculated in **(a)** suggests that the mean weight of pickles in a jar is above 454 g but interval calculated in **(b)** suggests that many individual jars will contain less than 454 g of pickles.

EXERCISE 6B

1 93.6–101.4.

2 **(a)** 812.2–883.8; **(b)** 831.3–864.7.

3 **(a)** 72.54–75.46;

    (b) No difficulty as sample is large so mean will be approximately normally distributed.

4 **(a)** **(i)** 2.717–2.755, **(ii)** 2.679–2.701; **(b)** 2.608–2.772;

    (c) Confidence intervals do not overlap so mean for soft centres clearly greater than mean for hard centres. However interval calculated in **(b)** shows that many hard-centred chocolates are bigger than the mean of the soft-centred chocolates. Diameter not a great deal of use because of large amount of overlap.

5 **(a)** 201.35–208.51; **(b)** **(i)** 0.150, **(ii)** 0.0265;

    (c) Average weight okay, too large a proportion less than 191 g and less than 182 g. This could be rectified by increasing the mean. Meeting the requirements in this way will mean that the mean contents are quite a lot over the nominal weight. Reducing the standard deviation is expensive but would allow the requirements to be met with a small reduction in the current mean contents.

EXERCISE 6C

1 (a) 266–516;

 (b) 0.1.

2 (a) (i) 2640–3080,
   (ii) 139;

 (b) (i) Some uncertainty as sample is small,
   (ii) No problem as sample is large;

 (c) Some doubt as if standard deviation is 300, the sample range is only about 1.5 standard deviations (or estimated standard deviation only 184).

3 (a) (i) 193.1–200.1,
   (ii) 195.1–198.1;

 (b) (i) 0.05,
   (ii) 0.05;

 (c) 0.02.

4 (a) 925–1092;

 (b) No substantial evidence of any difference;

 (c) 167;

 (d) 75.8;

 (e) 20.

7 Hypothesis testing

EXERCISE 7A

1 ts 1.80   cv 1.6449   mean greater than 135 kg.

2 ts −1.22   cv ±1.96   accept mean reaction time 7.5 s.

3 ts 1.05   cv 1.6449   accept children don't take longer.

4 ts −3.48   cv ±2.5758   mean length not satisfactory.

5 ts 1.67   cv 1.6449   silver not pure.

6 ts 3.19   cv 2.3263   mean weight has increased.

7 ts −1.57   cv −1.6449   mean weight not reduced.

8 ts 3.95   cv ±1.96   mean time greater than 4 s.

EXERCISE 7B

1 (a) (i) Conclude mean greater than 135 kg when in fact mean equals 135 kg,

   (ii) Conclude mean equals 135 kg when in fact mean greater than 135 kg;

(b) (i) 0.05,   **(ii)** 0.

2 (a) (i) Conclude mean unsatisfactory when it is satisfactory,

   (ii) Conclude mean is satisfactory when it is unsatisfactory;

(b) (i) 0.01,   **(ii)** 0.

3 (a) ts -1.80 cv ± 1.96 accept mean time is 20 minutes;

(b) Conclude mean time not 20 min when in fact it is 20 min;

(c) Would need to know the actual value of the mean.

4 (a) ts -1.69 cv ± 1.6449 mean length less than 19.25 mm;

(b) (i) Conclude mean not 19.25 mm when in fact it is 19.25 mm,

   (ii) Conclude mean 19.25 mm when in fact it is not 19.25 mm;

(c) 0.1.

5 (a) ts -1.90 cv -1.6449 easier to assemble;

(b) Conclude not easier to assemble when in fact it is.

EXERCISE 7C

1 ts 2.42   cv 2.3263   mean breaking strength greater than 195 kg.

2 ts 1.02   cv ± 1.96 mean resistance 1.5 Ω.

3 ts -2.67 cv -1.6449 mean test score lower.

4 ts 1.79   cv 1.6449   mean weight greater than 500 g.

5 ts -2.19 cv -2.3263 suspicions not correct.

Sample assumed random.

6 ts 1.87   cv 2.3263   mean weight not greater than 35 g.

7 (a) ts -4.98 cv -1.6449 mean less than 7.4;

(b) Test statistic is -4.98 so conclusion would have been unchanged even if the significance level had been very much less than 5%. Conclusion is very clear;

(c) As the sample is large it is not necessary to make any assumption about the distribution. However it is necessary to assume the sample is random. There is no information on this. If, for example, only those with particular symptoms had been tested they might be untypical of all varicoceles sufferers.

MIXED EXERCISE

1 ts -2.27 cv ± 1.96 readings biased.

2 ts 12.4 cv ± 2.5758 mean dust deposit greater than 60 g.

3 ts -2.11 cv -1.6449 mean score for new ice cream lower.

4 ts 2.14 cv 1.6449 mean higher than 77.4 mm.

5 ts 1.91 cv 1.6449 mean life longer.

6 (a) ts 3.19 cv ± 1.96 mean take home pay greater than £140;

  (b) (i) Large sample so conclusions not affected (central limit theorem),

   (ii) Conclusion unreliable – for example, whole sample could have been taken from one employer who paid relatively high wages.

7 (a) ts 1.54 cv 1.6449 mean mark not higher;

  (b) Mean of large sample approximately normally distributed by central limit theorem;

  (c) Sample was self selected. Probably children of highly motivated/gullible parents. Conclusion unreliable since sample not random.

Exam style practice paper

1 (a) (i) 0.81,

   (ii) 0.072;

  (b) 0.972;

  (c) (i) 0.009,

   (ii) 0.0576.

2 (a) (i) 0.195,

   (ii) 0.829;

  (b) 86.8 cm;

  (c) (i) Not valid – sample may be biased,

   (ii) Still valid. May assume mean of large sample is normally distributed. (Central Limit Theorem.)

3 (a) $z = 2.49$ cv 1.64 conclude applicants take longer than employees;

  (b) $z = 1.70$ cv 1.64 same conclusion.

4 (a)

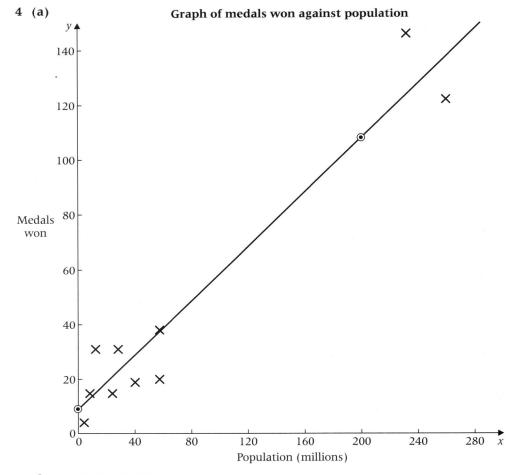

Graph of medals won against population

Medals won (y-axis), Population (millions) (x-axis)

(b) $y = 8.44 + 0.498x$;

(c) 83;

(d) Underestimate – Unified team won more medals than predicted by line, Russia is a large proportion of the population of countries making up the Unified team;

(e) 0.683;

(f) Fairly large positive correlation coefficient offers some support for suggestion that those countries which win a large number of medals at the Summer Games also tend to win a large number of medals at the Winter Games;

(g) Only countries which won at least four medals included, unified team made up of several countries, (other comments, e.g. no African countries, also acceptable).

5 (a) 0.292–1.41;

(b) Sample random, distribution normal;

(c) Outlier of 3.9 (or normal distribution with mean 1.01 and standard deviation 0.98 would give a substantial probability of negative distances) suggests distribution may not be normal;

(d) 0.874–1.15;

(e) Large sample so mean can be assumed to be normally distributed, sample stated to be random;

(f) 631.